Here are our options set before us: Option 1: A
Redeemer. Confidently trusting the Lord Jesus. Ser
"Treadmill" living. Running back to Mt. Sinai.
introspection. E. D. Burns proclaims Option 1 as t
the Great High Priest, and he also zeroes in on the biblical view of the love of God.
Such love, Burns argues, from the Triune God, motivates grateful and godly living.
Duplex Gratia, or the "double grace" of Jesus Christ, namely "Christ FOR us" and
"Christ IN us," permeate Burns's pen, resulting in a book that compels the reader to
keep reading.

MIKE ABENDROTH
Pastor, Bethlehem Bible Church, West Boylston, MA
Host, No Compromise Radio

This is a book that quite literally belongs in the hands of all believers. Every Christian
has either encountered this way of thinking in others, or even more likely, been
plagued themselves with such thoughts of a quid-pro-quo relationship with God.
Dr. Burns brings a stout assurance to believers of a right relationship with God, by
stripping away the infection of "karmic Christianity" and the prosperity gospel, in
turn, pointing us all to the singular hope that is found by faith alone in Christ alone.
Like a bright afternoon sun, it burns away the fog of fear, bondage, and groveling
servitude. May this book be used to bring freedom and a resting assurance to
myriads of precious saints whom Satan would seek to afflict with karma's lies.

BRIAN FAIRCHILD, DMin
Pastor, Colonial Bible Church, Midland, TX
Director, The Academy for Expository Preaching, OnePassion Ministries, Dallas, TX

With experience, clarity, and familiar examples, Burns explains a common thought
that can affect many of us in our faith, life, and service. The book moves between
well-researched insights and application. This book is not just about how others get
it wrong, but it presents help for each of us to see how we might set ourselves up
for unnecessary disappointment and exhaustion. The reader is led from thinking,
"if I—then God," to seeing and resting in the real, constant blessings from God.

INGEBJORG NANDRUP, MTh
Assistant Professor, Fjellhaug International University College, Oslo, Norway

In *Karmic Christianity*, E. D. Burns skillfully unmasks the deeper script that informs so much of evangelical Christianity today. While confessing the good news of grace-alone-by-faith-alone, far too many believers lapse into thinking that, ultimately, the "skeleton key" that guarantees success in the Christian life is, "enoughness"; intending well-enough, being good-enough, and working hard-enough. What attracts us to imagine that such a "karmic" transaction is the means to secure God's approval? I commend this book to the global church as a wake-up call to a pervasive and disturbing reality.

IVOR POOBALAN, PhD
Principal, Colombo Theological Seminary, Sri Lanka
Co-Chair of the Theology Working Group, Lausanne Movement

All too many people today are paralyzed by the counterfeit claims of *Karmic Christianity*. E. D. Burns seeks to correct these distortions of a transactional and contractual understanding with the liberating message of grace and faith in Jesus Christ. This helpful work can transform a person's anxiety about the spiritual life into assurance through resting in and living by God's promises.

TOM SCHWANDA, PhD
Associate Professor Emeritus of Christian Formation and Ministry, Wheaton College

Karmic Christianity

Finding Peace by Faith Alone

E. D. Burns

WILLIAM CAREY PUBLISHING
visit us at missionbooks.org

William Carey Publishing (WCP) publishes resources to shape and advance the missiological conversation in the world. We publish a broad range of thought-provoking books and do not necessarily endorse all opinions set forth here or in works referenced within this book. WCP can't verify the accuracy of website URLs beyond the date of print publication.

Published by William Carey Publishing
10 W. Dry Creek Cir
Littleton, CO 80120 | www.missionbooks.org

William Carey Publishing is a ministry of Frontier Ventures
Pasadena, CA | www.frontierventures.org

Cover and Interior Designer: Mike Riester

ISBNs: 978-1-64508-507-2 (paperback)
       978-1-64508-509-6 (epub)

Printed Worldwide
27 26 25 24 23   1 2 3 4 5   IN

Library of Congress Control Number: 2023941921

Dedicated to:

Ben, a friend who sticks closer than a brother,
whose affection and loyalty are more than I deserve.

*To be convinced in our hearts
that we have forgiveness of sins
and peace with God by grace alone
is the hardest thing.*

—Martin Luther

Contents

Foreword

What does karma have to do with Christianity? At first glance, the title of this book might seem odd. The eastern religious idea of cosmic cause and effect seems far removed from the truth that we are saved by grace alone through faith alone in Christ alone. And that is the point. In this little but powerful book, E. D. Burns takes on a major problem afflicting evangelical believers around the world today. The idea of karma has become a stow away in the lives of many Christians as they proceed on their journey to the heavenly city. Though they know that they are ultimately saved by grace and not by works, there is confusion about the role of their own good works in receiving blessings in this present life. How can I get God's blessings? Why is God withholding blessings? Is it something I have done? Is there something I have failed to do? What is the key to unlock the windows of heaven so God's blessings will pour down?

Because these sorts of questions and doubts plague many believers, they live in a state of uncertainty. They know God loves them but wonder if they are doing enough to serve him. They question if they have enough faith. The problem is compounded by well-meaning churches and preachers who claim that if we just obeyed God more, then greater levels of personal and even national blessings will follow. It is claimed that our lack of faith, or doing enough, or doing the right things is the bottleneck preventing us from receiving God's best for us. But as Burns explains, that mentality is more related to karma than Christianity, and it needs to be rooted out of the Christian's life.

This book is not the first book to address the topics of grace versus works, or the source of the Christian's peace and assurance. But in a day of activism and division about the nature and scope of the gospel, and the mission of the church, Burns provides a timely and succinct call to believers to resist the temptation to endless anxious toil in pursuit of greater blessings. Too many Christians have misunderstood the proverbial wisdom of Scripture as contractual promises whereby God is obliged to bless us if only we have enough faith and faithfulness. But how much is enough? When do you know? The focus of the Christian life should not be about grace for salvation after death and good works for blessings in this life. That is not how it works.

Though our actions do have consequences, God is not trying to keep his blessings just out of reach until we are able to jump high enough to snatch them out of his hand.

In these pages, Burns points readers to key biblical truths in order to lift the heavy burden off of their minds and shoulders so that they may rest in the new covenant peace that Christ has given to them. Trusting in the finished work of Christ is sufficient for receiving all that God has for us in this life and in eternity. We need not labor under the fear that if we were just doing something more or something different, then (and only then!) will we experience or achieve all that God has for us. Burns ably reminds us that in God's providence, we each experience sufferings and blessings according to his sovereign plan for us so that we might trust him and see his glory. God is in charge, and we need not constantly wonder if we are holding up his plans.

The message of peace and confidence in God's goodness and in the work of Christ that Burns presents is an important reminder for Christians today when so many believers around the world are anxious about God's blessings (or lack thereof). Whether it is the passionate worshipper seeking deeper spiritual experiences, or the committed activist trying to transform the culture, or the modern puritan seeking internal and external purity, the message is the same. Rest in God's goodness. Trust in the finished work of Christ. Serve Christ without fear.

As fallen human beings we are all inclined towards a karmic, or works-based, mentality but this book is a message of freedom and peace that lifts high the gospel of Christ as the heavenly balm of peace for our fears and doubts in an age of anxious toil. The peace of God and the kingdom of God are gifts. They cannot be earned by doing better or being better, and they cannot be lost by failing to be good enough or to do enough. Jesus is enough.

It is my hope and prayer that if you are laboring in anxious toil and wonder if you are doing enough, in the pages that follow you will find peace and freedom as Burns skillfully directs our hearts and minds to the only one who is enough, our only Lord and Savior Jesus Christ.

REV. KARL DAHLFRED, PhD
Professor, Chiang Mai Theological Seminary (Thailand)
Missionary, OMF International

Preface

This book is the overflow of many of my writings and lectures. I have taught for years on the topic of peace and fear, but I have never distilled it into a book like this one. Throughout this book, I will reference some of my previous writings so that readers who wish to may study the issues that I don't address fully in this volume.

This work is not designed to be an academic book or a missions book, though I am both a professor and a missionary. My desire is that this book will be helpful, encouraging, and applicable. Some advanced theological language and biblical exegesis will be omitted. I don't exegete texts or cite historical sources that I would normally use in a classroom, but hopefully, this will be more accessible than a heavy academic or theological discussion.

I wrote this book for global Christians who deeply desire to know God and make him known but fear they are never good enough. I will use allusions and examples from popular Western culture in the Global North, but hopefully the illustrations are clear enough that anyone in the Global South can benefit as well. This book will also use American spelling and the *English Standard Version* of the Bible.

E. D. Burns
Southeast Asia
June 2023

Introduction

Fear and Peace

Scripture for Memory
For the kingdom of God is not a matter of eating and drinking but of righteousness and peace and joy in the Holy Spirit. (Rom 14:17)

"You really should write down what God is teaching you so that you don't have to go through this again or something worse."

Jon nodded and smiled after receiving this advice from a Christian leader. He was devastated by misunderstandings and misrepresentations of his character. Jon was in his first year of full-time ministry, and he had been placed on a ministry team that did not align with his theological convictions or ministry principles. Jon and his wife soon realized that they didn't ask the right questions about the team leaders before joining. They assumed too much about their common passions for the ministry location and needs. Jon's wife also developed an autoimmune disorder within three months of starting the ministry project—he couldn't keep up with the demands of the ministry and the unknowns of his wife's health. He and his wife eventually decided to change locations and projects for the sake of her health and long-term viability in ministry.

Though his ministry supervisors granted him permission, the transition wasn't as smooth as Jon anticipated. He tried to abide by his church's doctrinal statement, but the ministry he was working for was far too relaxed on some essential points. He was labeled a theological nitpicker by some leaders overseeing his transition, which through the rumor mill of emails between supervisors became slanderous accusations of divisiveness, insubordination to authority, and doctrinaire arrogance. No one could actually point to a specific sin in Jon. But they would often talk about how his Bible knowledge often made them feel judged and criticized.

Jon later found out that people had been talking about how he was walking outside of God's umbrella of protection. "What does that mean?" Jon wondered. He found out that his ministry project leaders viewed blind obedience to spiritual authorities as essential for receiving God's blessings in life and ministry. If Jon were to express a minority opinion on issues of ministry preference, theological emphasis, or scriptural application, he would be charged with quenching the Holy Spirit. How so? Jon and his home church believed God spoke through his written word, but the organization's supervisors believed God spoke through impressions, promptings, dreams, visions, prophecies, anointed leaders, and other extra-biblical means. Every time he bristled at obeying his leaders' prophetic words, the blessings of God vanished. He would only know God's rod and chastisement.

Moreover, his wife's newly diagnosed autoimmune disorder seemed to consume her. One day, a supervisor hinted that Jon's lack of enthusiasm in obeying his chain of command might have led to his wife's illness. Jon felt gut-punched. Was it true? Did he do this to his wife? Was God punishing him for just trying to follow Scripture (and his ministry ordination vows) over against the frequently changing spiritual impressions and special revelations of his superiors? Did he miss God's will? Did he join the wrong team? God must have sent him some signs; how could he have missed them all? What must he do to fix it? Would God eventually change his mind and heal his wife? When would Jon's efforts to reverse the cryptic scolding be enough? Fear consumed him. He knew no peace.

What Does Karma Have to Do with It?

Don't be alarmed. This book is not promoting karma. The title is supposed to provoke and create curiosity. It's designed to stick with you so that you are more conscious of how easy it is to slip into a karmic relationship with the Lord. The fact is that most Christians around the world are unaware of how much they think, feel, and live in a karmic system. I am not using "karma" in the traditional Buddhist sense, relating to merits and reincarnation. Rather, my use of "karma" refers to the more popular, worldly spirituality that tries to attach spiritual meaning or spiritual causes to good and bad experiences, blessings and hardships. Here is how I have defined this idea elsewhere:

This propensity to discern God's degree of pleasure over your life based upon how much or how little He seems to be blessing you is what I call "karmic Christianity." This mindset is not original to Eastern religions. It is a human problem. Karmic Christianity is the Christianized temptation to diagnose all the consequences of the curse in this life with remedies of doing more or doing better in order to secure fruitfulness, inner peace, life-giving relationships, physical health, financial stability, and an overall sense that God finally approves of your efforts now. He seems to like you more now that you are sincere and serious about your relationship with Him. You can rest assured. Good things are on the way.[1]

Fear and Peace, not Fear and Power

It has become a standard assumption in most missional literature that there are community-oriented honor/shame cultures that many in the West have overlooked or not adequately noticed. Along with the rising popularity of this notion is the parallel suggestion that other cultures are more marked by a fear/power paradigm. This idea presumes that fear/power cultures seek power (e.g., *Christus Victor*) as the solution to their fear problem. I don't disagree with this application completely, but it is fundamentally flawed. As I've demonstrated,

> Some missiologists allege that since demons inflict harm and cause fear, then spiritualistic people desire *power* to overcome such demon-induced dread. True, to be set free from demonic oppression we need a power greater than ourselves. But power is essentially a *means* for reaching peace, and that's what we all finally want. And in karmic cultures, the prevalence of fear and desire for peace are palpable. Fear and peace theologically and textually often overlap. … Fear and power, though popularly used in missiological conversations, do not correspond conceptually or biblically. Fear is a subjective feeling rooted in a threat. And though power may mitigate the threat, power is not the ultimate subjective replacement of fear. Peace is. Power and strength are qualities of condition, like their common antitheses—weakness and vulnerability. Sometimes people in spiritualistic orientations are quite aware of the evil spirits around

1 E. D. Burns, *Seeds and Stars: Resting in Christ for Great Commission Service* (Cape Coral, FL: Founders Press, 2023), 100.

them, especially in the temples and sacred sites. But their conscious daily experience is not so fixated on the presence of the demons as it is on the *lies* of demons that haunt their thinking. Such lies impact their temptations to sin, superstitions, and anxious decision-making. So it is, also, with karma-background Christians. ... The fear they suffer most is not so much from regular manifest encounters with evil spirits as much as from believing doctrines of demons that the gospel of peace has yet to vanquish.[2]

I first started ministering among Buddhist-background people in 2002, and then later with karmic-background believers. The ministry opportunities God provided took me around the world to serve in very diverse contexts from remote to urban, animistic to atheistic, and polytheistic to monotheistic. I noticed that local Christians in each of these contexts struggled to maintain God's blessing in their lives (as they perceived it) and to avoid adversity. Moreover, I realized I was just like them. In our own ways, we were all anxious or fearful of displeasing the Lord and then learning the hard way. But this was not merely a healthy fear of falling into grievous sin and suffering direct consequences (e.g., committing adultery and losing your marriage). This was an unsettling fear of not knowing enough, being enough, or doing enough to warrant and maintain God's temporal blessings.

Sometimes this looks like going on a short-term missions trip, tithing more generously, heading up a ministry in church, or praising more passionately with all our heart. And when we have done enough to feel God's presence, we begin to look for signs of God's favor and blessing. When something good comes along, we smile, "God is good, all the time. All the time, God is good." We can observe this tendency in our fear of making decisions without knowing God's perfect will or hearing God's leading. So, we pray and pray, wait and wait, and many of us are paralyzed with fear of missing out on God's best for us. After all, you only live once. Don't settle for second best. So, what is the answer? Not power. We want peace. Inner peace. We want the uneasy feelings to go away so we can be still and know that he is God. We want to know that he likes us again.

But then, something unforeseen happens. Our fears are realized. Maybe your fiancé cheated on you and broke your heart. Maybe you had

2 E. D. Burns, *Ancient Gospel, Brave New World: Jesus Still Saves Sinners in Cultures of Shame, Fear, Bondage, and Weakness* (Cape Coral, FL: Founders Press, 2022), 280–81.

your third miscarriage. Maybe you lost your job, again. Maybe it's cancer. The bogeyman in your closet has come out to torment you. What were potential threats yesterday are present terrors today. Our dreams prove fake while our nightmares prove real. It must be that God's blessings are being withdrawn because he needs to teach us a lesson. We should have paid better attention the first time. Or maybe we were never that special to him in the first place. What is so wrong with us that we just can't do enough to get back under his umbrella of protection? If we could just work up enough believing faith, then we could pray successfully for healing. Or, if we could just unite the church with enough faith-filled prayer (with no one doubting in their hearts), align lockstep with God's perfect plans, then we could bind the evil spirits that are wreaking havoc in our lives. If we could just map their strongholds, we could rebuke the demons so that God's blessings could be released again. Maybe if we gave a widow's mite, then God might be pleased enough to help us pay our rent. Our own lack of faith has probably caused this whole mess. If we could follow the promptings of his Spirit, hear Jesus calling, let go and let God, obey God's chain of command, and just have faith, then we could tip the scales in our favor and secure God's promises.

God has blessings in heaven ready to be loosed. If we would only believe with true faith, then they could be ours. If … then, if … then. What is that? That's karma. It's a contractual religion. A transactional religion. This mindset does not characterize a secure relationship with the faithful covenant-keeping God of the Bible. No, this is a shallow relationship with a fickle contract-making genie of our own fallen human experience. We subconsciously (and sometimes even consciously) project upon God how we have perceived the authorities in our life—that imperfect father who wounded our little hearts, that irritable supervisor who was impossible to keep happy, that indulgent grandfather who was too frail to do much to help us, or that narcissistic pastor whose whole ministry seemed to use people until they got in his way. This is all a Christian version of karma. Karmic Christianity is the common mode of interpreting God's mysterious providences of blessing and discipline through contractual stipulations and transactional rituals. It's a reap-what-you-sow, tit-for-tat religion of retribution. If we think, feel, or do this enough, then God will do that. But if you don't, then count your blessings because there won't be any more until you're good enough again.

Though this is the normal Christian experience for many of us, it doesn't need to be this way. There is gospel hope for the struggler. You can know the peace of God and rest in the harbor of his sovereign grace. You can be still and know that he is God. Peace. Safety. Rest. Assurance.

Main Point

As you read this book, I pray that the Holy Spirit plants the following truths in your hearts and minds: All the promises of God are ours in Christ Jesus. Yet, in this life some Christians will enjoy temporary blessings seemingly more than others. But this reality is not a result of favoritism on God's part; rather, in God's providence, he exercises his wisdom, benevolence, and sovereignty in mysterious ways to conform us all to Christ. The true blessed life will be realized in the resurrection. The Bible says, "Just as David also speaks of the blessing of the one to whom God counts righteousness apart from works: 'Blessed are those who lawless deeds are forgiven, and whose sins are covered; blessed is the man against whom the Lord will not count his sin," (Rom 4:6–8; cf. Ps 32:1–2). It does not say, "Blessed is the one who has infrequent and small transgression." It does not say, "Blessed is the one whose sin is under control." It does not say, "Blessed is the one whose faithfulness is good enough." Rather, it says that the only basis for receiving God's blessings is the imputed righteousness of Christ for those who trust in him. Being and doing good enough to keep the potential blessings of God's contract is not Christianity. It's karma. It's conditional. It's a fear-based system.

Instead, Christians should rest in Christ who earned all the promised blessings of God's covenant with us. God's perfect love casts out our fear. We are at peace with God. Our unshakeable security is based upon Christ's performance for us in life and in death. Jesus is our "peace from God" (Rom 1:7), our "peace with God" (Rom 5:1), and our "Peace in God" (Phil 4:7). Jesus is our Prince of Peace (Isa 9:6).

Karma seeks to achieve potential blessings. Christianity rests to receive promised blessings. Karma works by a contract. Christianity rests in a covenant. Karma worries that God is punishing us in arbitrary adversity. Christianity trusts that God is purifying us in mysterious providence. Karma works at the base of Sinai in fear. Christianity dwells within the gates of Zion in peace.

Goal of This Book

My prayer is simply that this book will restore hope and peace to troubled souls who stagger under the weight of their own karmic constructs. Karmic Christianity is essentially the performance-based contract of Sinai, not the grace-based liberty of Zion. This book employs the Protestant Reformation's law/gospel framework in its application. As the Reformation taught, the stipulations of the law covenant promise blessing, only for perfect, perpetual, and personal obedience. But Jesus is the better Adam and the better Israel who fulfilled the law's demand for obedience and penalty for disobedience. Jesus joyfully became a servant to those who trust in him. He is their righteousness. The great Christmas hymn rejoices that "He comes to make his blessings flow far as the curse is found," while another famous hymn celebrates that "His law is love and His gospel is peace." For those united with Christ through faith alone, he has secured all the promises of God and their eternal blessings. My aim is to help the reader realize the pervasive karmic trappings in much of our Christian spirituality. More than that, I want to encourage restfulness of soul. May you have a glad-hearted contentment in God that laughs at the days to come. May you know that if you are in Christ, all is well. If God is for us, who or what can be against us? Fear not. God loves you.

Audience

Though I write from the perspective of a someone in full-time ministry with academic education and cross-cultural service, my intended audience is the global church—all those Christians who care deeply about walking with God in faithfulness but who struggle to make sense of the mysterious and sometimes severe providences of God. This book is for those who feel anxious and afraid of either messing up or not doing enough to ensure God's blessings. This book is for the secret struggler. This book is also for those who embody the victorious life—those who love to give unsolicited advice to the struggler.

Rest in Your Shepherd

As you read this book, reflect honestly on your misunderstandings and misapplications of Scripture and your knowledge of God. It's impossible to convey everything I would like to say in this book, especially all those truths I have learned over the years that have contributed to my sanctification in the Spirit. I have done nothing perfectly, and even this book, with all my best efforts will fall short. But I am confident that the gospel of peace can calm your anxious soul as it does for me every day. Our God is love, and love is neither irritable nor does it keep a record of wrongs (1 Cor 13:5). Let the perfect love of God cast out your fear (1 John 4:18). May you know deeply the peace of resting in the sovereign grace that God provided on a bloody Roman cross two thousand years ago. Let Jesus lead you beside still water. Let Jesus restore your soul (Ps 23:2, 3).

Hymn for Reflection

"Arise, My Soul, Arise"[3]

1 Arise, my soul, arise,
shake off your guilty fears;
the bleeding Sacrifice
in my behalf appears.
Before the throne my Surety stands,
before the throne my Surety stands;
my name is written on his hands,
my name is written on his hands.

2 He ever lives above,
for me to intercede,
his all-redeeming love,
his precious blood to plead.
His blood atoned for ev'ry race,
his blood atoned for ev'ry race,
and sprinkles now the throne of grace,
and sprinkles now the throne of grace.

---

3 Charles Wesley, "Arise, My Soul, Arise," https://hymnary.org/text/arise_my_soul_arise_ shake_off_thy_guilty.

3 Five bleeding wounds he bears,
received on Calvary;
they pour effectual prayers,
they strongly plead for me.
"Forgive him, O forgive," they cry,
"forgive him, O forgive," they cry,
"nor let that ransomed sinner die,
nor let that ransomed sinner die!"

4 My God is reconciled;
his pard'ning voice I hear.
He owns me for his child,
I can no longer fear.
with confidence I now draw nigh,
with confidence I now draw nigh,
and "Father, Abba, Father!" cry,
and "Father, Abba, Father!" cry.

Questions for Reflection

1. How has this brief introduction to karmic expressions of Christianity made you reflect on your own life as a Christian?

2. What area of Christian life, growth, or service is a struggle for you?

3. What is one take-away from this introduction on peace and fear that you could share with someone to encourage them?

Chapter 1

Karma and God's Purposes

"God, what did I do to deserve this?" Olivia sobbed as her hopes and dreams vanished in a moment. Her husband had broken her heart, again. He was her high school sweetheart, her pastor's son, and she would never forget how godly he seemed in youth group and how dominant he was on the football field. After high school, Jackson enlisted in the military, and Olivia busily served the Lord in a Zambian orphanage. After his first tour and Olivia's stint in Zambia, they returned to their small town and married. Yet something was different about Jackson. A secret drinking problem he hid away in high school followed him to the frontlines and back home. Olivia would find him drinking late into the night, and she'd scold him back to sobriety for a while. But tonight, she didn't catch him in time—Jackson crashed his car. With the sirens still ringing in her ears, she stared in the bathroom mirror at a new widow. A month later, Olivia would miscarry their first baby. She wondered where she missed God's will. All the signs of blessing were there: Jackson was the youth group's passionate worship leader, the football team's record-breaking quarterback, and the hometown war hero. Olivia was the church's esteemed missionary to Africa. But she seemed to have missed the Lord's perfect will, and now she was paying for it.

Samantha, on the other hand, Olivia's twin sister, was a chronic struggler. Occasionally she'd slip out of high school youth group to smoke weed. She dropped out of high school her senior year to work at the mall with her boyfriend. She'd move in with a new guy every year or so and then go to church during holidays to pacify her parents' angst. Samantha lived in the fast lane. The rush of playing the rebel was a thrill. But one day, her world came crashing down. She overheard a Christian song playing in a coffee shop. It was a song she used to sing in youth group whenever she would attend. Something shifted deep in her soul. All her sins flashed before her mind, and the gospel messages she blew off in youth group flooded her conscience. By the time she got home, Samantha, through her tears, was praising Jesus for saving her soul. The year after Olivia miscarried and was widowed, Samantha gave birth to twin sons after marrying a godly man who worked for her father. At her baby shower, Olivia grimaced. She knew envy and hate were sinful, but they seemed like the only just emotions. How in the world did her prodigal sister deserve such blessings? What was so wrong with Olivia that God would punish her so severely? Was God trustworthy? Was he good? Did God have favorites? What did Samantha do to change God's mind and get all her blessings? How was Olivia not good enough? This just wasn't fair.

Good Luck or Finding God's Will?

There's something about underdog stories that attract our attention, whether they be about shepherd boys slaying giants or humble hobbits carrying a coveted ring to Mount Doom. Sometimes we are tempted to envy those who, against all odds, seem to find the secrets to success and satisfaction—great jobs, great families, great vacations, great relationships with the Lord. Sometimes we want to imitate them because there's something they must have done differently with their lives that brought about so much of God's blessings. So we listen carefully for hints on how they eat, exercise, do their devotions, parent their children, date their spouse, build their careers, and so on.

We can subconsciously assume that the successful person whom we idealize so much has somehow tapped into the secret of God's will. What is it about that person that God loves to bless? At church they raise their hands in passionate worship. Maybe they truly love God with their whole heart—

radical surrender, abandoned devotion, crazy love. They could sing of God's love forever, and indeed they probably do.

These people are attractive—healthy bodies, charming personalities, happy families, immaculate houses, and stable finances. Their life song seems to go something like, "Jesus loves me this I know, for my blessings tell me so." We wonder what lucky charm they picked up along the way. We observe secret clues to God's favor over them: daily Bible reading, homeschooling, classical education, organic foods, music lessons, Christian radio, positive and upbeat demeanor, hearing God's voice, sweet intimacy with Jesus, and the list goes on. We call it "finding God's will," "walking in the Spirit," "living in obedience," or simply "following Jesus."

All these labels are code for "good karma." It's a transactional religion. Good things happen to good-enough-Christians. Like most parents, God has favorites among his children. And he blesses those who know how to move his heart.

Bad Luck or Missing God's Will?

Nevertheless, there are those times when Christians go through repeated trials—maybe cancer, a financial loss, a house fire, and the like. Maybe that's you. For a time, you even seemed happy and successful. But a switch was flipped in your life. Instinctively, you slowly conclude that God is disciplining you for something that you need to figure out. You don't want to miss the lesson and then repeat the same test. Unlike those you've observed who hear the voice of the Spirit and soak in Jesus's special love, you don't radiate the same dreamy sentimentality for Jesus. In fact, people think you can be downright plain—even a bit dour sometimes.

You play the game of comparisons. There are the *haves* and *have-nots*. Not only are you a *have-not*, but you're also a *has-been*. You once had God's ear. His eyes were on you, and you loved to sing his praises. But after the miscarriage and job loss, you've done some soul searching. Is God trying to get your attention now? But for what? Was it because you enrolled your child in public school? Maybe it was because you secretly doubted when people at church prayed so passionately for you. You didn't have enough faith. Could it have been that you married the wrong person? You know you shouldn't have been talking to singles online. You should have followed your pastor's advice to only date within your church. Maybe the cancer is because you didn't take advantage of God's natural foods and remedies. And the worst of it is that your personal Bible study has slipped. Your prayer life feels dry. You say it's because you're a busy parent and your health has declined. But you beat yourself up inside. You know you've failed God. You've departed God's perfect will. You stop investing in God's will, and your spiritual portfolio of blessings becomes obsolete.

Again, here is another version of transactional religion. This is all code for "bad karma." Bad things happen to not-good-enough Christians. You were one of God's favorites, and you knew it when you'd feel the surge of passion during summer camp. But you no longer impress him. He is over you now and has moved on. Sure, he loves you. But he probably doesn't like you as much anymore.

To play off an iconic cultural analogy, the Eagles' anthem of the 1970s captured well what it can feel like to get stuck in an endless cycle. Welcome to "hotel karmafornia": "We are all just prisoners here, of our own device." "This could be heaven or this could be hell." "You can check out any time you like, but you can never leave."

Job's Friends and God's Faithfulness

If you've ever received counsel from a pastor, parent, or fellow Christian about discerning God's voice and what he might be teaching or showing you during a time of severe trial, you might have felt confused and frustrated. Maybe even unfairly treated. You couldn't control the lies and misrepresentations that were hurled at you, and their social media posts spread like wildfire. To add insult to injury, you totaled your car in an accident that was not your fault. Now you limp around with a fractured leg. But really, you limp around with a fractured soul because the advice you've received consists of calling you to discern what God might be saying to you. You better learn your lesson so you don't have to go through this again. Whatever it is, it must be deeply lodged in your life, since this is what it took for God to weed it out.

Inevitably, the navel-gazing and dizzying introspection begins. As your world spins out of control, the unsolicited comments and advice keep beating you up. It's all done in the name of Christian love and pastoral care, of course. And to be fair, most people who say such ridiculous things truly think they are helping. If we're honest, we've all probably said similar things to others or even to ourselves. But in fact, none of us understand the mysterious providences of God. We are unwittingly binding the conscience and going beyond Scripture. Partly out of immaturity, partly out of presumption, and partly out of unbiblical advice we have also received.

Similarly, as Job's friends gave him a mixture of naïve opinions, decent theology with bad application, and just plain tit-for-tat religion, they missed the point. They assumed that Job, who on the surface appeared to be a righteous man, must have harbored a secret sin that God was now exposing. But when they couldn't accuse him of anything that would stick, they left the interpretation of God's severity for Job to decipher. They're hands were clean. They did their duty in admonishing Job. Apparently, he had made his bed, and he was going to sleep in it. In other words, you reap what you sow. Job's friends are the classic karmic counselors. Such people assign secret sins and bad motives to chronic strugglers whose suffering has no relevant correlation to a known sin.

Keep in mind that rejecting a karmic view of Christianity doesn't mean that you are always innocent and that God has nothing to teach you in your adversity. Neither does it mean that patterns of obedience don't generally contribute to good outcomes. We must be careful not to interpret every affliction as a sign of God's disapproval, but we must also be careful not to harden ourselves against the blessing of God's fatherly discipline in hardship. For those united to Christ, God uses affliction for our good. Always. Even if that affliction is an actual direct consequence of sin, God's disposition toward us in Christ is always grace and blessing. God may indeed bring good from fatherly chastisement in producing a humble and repentant heart. But discipline is always a form of purification and never punishment. Never. As the Scripture says, "There is therefore now no condemnation for those who are in Christ Jesus" (Rom 8:1).

Nevertheless, we must stop trying to decode the mysterious providences of God in our pain and even in our blessings as though we can control them if we can only locate their triggers. We need to stop assuming we can figure out God's purposes this side of heaven. The issue here is not that wicked choices are without consequence. There are indeed temporal consequences for sin, like draining your finances with a gambling addiction, crashing your car while driving drunk, or losing your marriage because of adultery. That's why there are incalculable warnings in Scripture about fleeing sin and pursing righteousness. Play stupid games, win stupid prizes.

But Job's friends insert themselves in the place of God and decode the puzzles of providence and give the special meaning to struggling saints. They are good enough theologians to say many correct proverbial principles, but they often misapply their theology in their overly confident interpretation of Job's suffering. And Job rightly stuck it to his karmic accusers:

> As for you, you whitewash with lies; worthless physicians are you all. Oh that you would keep silent, and it would be your wisdom! Hear now my argument and listen to the pleadings of my lips. Will you speak falsely for God and speak deceitfully for him? … Your maxims are proverbs of ashes; your defenses are defenses of clay. (Job 13:4–7, 12)

As Job's resolve to defend himself deteriorated, he began to question God's wisdom, purposes, and power. God patiently yet firmly responded to Job. Instead of consuming Job, he corrected Job with a vision of his sovereign power. Consider a snapshot of God's rebuttal:

"Dress for action like a man; I will question you, and you make it known to me. Will you even put me in the wrong? Will you condemn me that you may be in the right? Have you an arm like God, and can you thunder with a voice like his?" (Job 40:7–9). And after two chapters of God making known his sovereign power, Job humbly confessed:

> I know that you can do all things, and that no purpose of yours can be thwarted. "Who is this that hides counsel without knowledge?" Therefore I have uttered what I did not understand, things too wonderful for me, which I did not know. "Hear, and I will speak; I will question you, and you make it known to me." I had heard of you by the hearing of the ear, but now my eye sees you; therefore I despise myself, and repent in dust and ashes. (Job 42:2–6)

And what was God's take on the karmic advice of Job's friends? Was it, "They meant well. You just need to listen for a kernel of truth in their feedback"? Hardly. God's anger burned that they would go beyond God's revealed word and speak confidently of the mysterious purposes of God: "My anger burns against you and against your two friends, for you have not spoken of me what is right, as my servant Job has" (Job 42:7).

What did Job say from the beginning and throughout the letter that was so right? At the first devastating losses, Job would declare, "The LORD gave, and the LORD has taken away; blessed be the name of the LORD" (Job 1:21). And lest we are tempted to correct Job's theology and inform him that Satan did it and that God is so good that he wouldn't ever ordain such a thing, the next verse gives a commentary: "In all this Job did not sin or charge God with wrong" (Job 1:22). Job would acquiesce, "Though he slay me, I will hope in him" (Job 13:15). Why hope in God in the slaughter? "For I know that my Redeemer lives, and at the last he will stand upon the earth. And after my skin has been thus destroyed, yet in my flesh I shall see God, whom I shall see for myself, and my eyes shall behold, and not another" (Job 19:25–27). Job's hope was in resurrection. All of God's bitter providences would only make sense when Job would stand in his flesh on the earth and see his Redeemer in the flesh standing before him. Then, and only then, would it all make sense. And it would be worth it. Every temporary loss would be translated into everlasting gain—an immense weight of the glory of the grace of God. An avalanche of lavish kindness so consuming that only a resurrected body in the new creation could withstand it.

Lest we think that God forgets all our losses, he gave Job in his latter days double of what he lost in the beginning. He lost seven thousand sheep, three thousand camels, five hundred yoke of oxen and five hundred female donkeys, and received fourteen thousand sheep, six thousand camels, one thousand yoke of oxen, and one thousand female donkeys. More importantly, Job lost seven sons and three daughters. But what is interesting is that God gave him seven sons and three daughters again. Why double the animals but not double the children? What gives? Is God fickle, saying one thing but doing another? Had Job still not learned all his lessons completely?

God indeed gave Job double the offspring; Job's initial seven sons and three daughters and his second set of seven sons and three daughters will join him in the resurrection. The story of Job is shot through with resurrection hope. God's purposes are infinitely higher than our perspectives. We see only the present and control nothing; God sees the past, present, and future simultaneously and controls everything. He always plays 3D chess, as it were, and is ten thousand moves ahead of us. As William Cowper's famous hymn affirms,

Judge not the Lord by feeble sense,
But trust him for his grace;
Behind a frowning providence
He hides a smiling face.[1]

---

1 William Cowper, "God Moves in a Mysterious Way," https://hymnary.org/text/god_moves_in_a_mysterious_way.

Jesus Rebukes Karmic Ideas

The propensity to interpret peculiar suffering as directly connected to some secret lesson we must learn or some secret sin we must forsake is all part of the fallen human condition. As is the tendency to assume that a Christian's unique blessings are directly connected to God's favoritism or special reward for extraordinary obedience. We don't need to be taught to perceive reality this way. It comes naturally. It's part of our fallen human outlook. Consider the Apostle Paul who survived a shipwreck during a terrible storm and washed up on the island of Malta. He was later bitten by a viper, and the islanders automatically presumed Paul had a well-deserved destiny with death: "When the native people saw the creature hanging from his hand, they said to one another, 'No doubt this man is a murderer. Though he escaped from the sea, Justice has not allowed him to live'" (Acts 28:4). Seeing life through the lens of karma is as ancient as human sin.

Consider even how Jesus's disciples, who were well educated in Jewish theology, interpreted strange providences like birth defects: "As he passed by, he saw a man blind from birth. And his disciples asked him, 'Rabbi, who sinned, this man or his parents, that he was born blind'" (John 9:1–2). Notice how Jesus answered. He did not say, "Well, his parents were living in sin before marriage, and God needed to teach them a lesson," or "God would have never allowed this, but he can still somehow turn it for his glory." No. Jesus answered with confidence in the purpose of God: "It was not that this man sinned, or his parents, but that the works of God might be displayed in him" (John 9:3). And then Jesus healed the blind man. Since it was the Sabbath, the religious leaders were enraged. They pressed the healed man to admit what happened. To their dismay, the man testified to the divinity of Christ, thus displaying the works of God to spiritually blind people: "Never since the world began has it been heard that anyone opened the eyes of a man born blind. If this man were not from God, he could do nothing" (John 9:32, 33). There, in that commotion, Jesus showed that it was not sin directly committed by the parents or the man that made him blind. It was for a purpose—so that the works of God would be displayed in Christ: "The LORD opens the eyes of the blind" (Ps 146:8).

Jesus also attacked head-on the karmic interpretation of catastrophe. He rebuked the idea of extraordinary suffering being commensurately attached to extraordinary sin. In Luke 13:1–5, Jesus was clear that those who escape disaster ought to repent of sin just as much as those who perish:

> There were some present at that very time who told him about the Galileans whose blood Pilate had mingled with their sacrifices. And he answered them, "Do you think that these Galileans were worse sinners than all the other Galileans, because they suffered in this way? No, I tell you; but unless you repent, you will all likewise perish. Or those eighteen on whom the tower in Siloam fell and killed them: do you think that they were worse offenders than all the others who lived in Jerusalem? No, I tell you; but unless you repent, you will all likewise perish."

He Commands the Wind and the Waves

Understanding the truth that suffering and blessings are not directly connected to man's sin should not imply that hell is random or that eternal punishment is unrelated to degrees of wickedness in this life. The simple reality is that on the temporal plain of life this side of death, there is not always a one-to-one correlation between our sin and our suffering. Why might a child die in a car wreck on an icy road the same night on the other side of the city a drunk driver makes it home safely? Why has God allowed unspeakable degeneracy to accelerate in our day but quickly vaporized Sodom? His sovereign purposes in this earthly life are often shrouded in secrecy, but eternity will reveal the manifold wisdom and righteousness of God. "God is his own interpreter. He will make it plain."[2]

Sometimes God churns up a storm to remind us how small we are. "I am the LORD your God, who stirs up the sea so that its waves roar" (Isa 51:15). "You rule the raging of the sea; when its waves rise, you still them" (Ps 89:9).

> And [Jesus] awoke and rebuked the wind and said to the sea, "Peace! Be still!" And the wind ceased, and there was a great calm. He said to them, "Why are you so afraid? Have you still no faith?" And they were filled with great fear and said to one another, "Who then is this, that even the wind and the sea obey him?" (Mark 4:39–41)

Jesus stirs up and stills the tempest that we might stand in fearful awe and inquire, "Who is this?"

---

2 William Cowper, "God Moves in a Mysterious Way," https://hymnary.org/text/god_moves_in_a_mysterious_way.

Hymn for Reflection

"God Moves in a Mysterious Way"[3]

1 God moves in a mysterious way
His wonders to perform.
He plants his footsteps in the sea
And rides upon the storm.

2 You fearful saints, fresh courage take;
The clouds you so much dread
Are big with mercy and shall break
In blessings on your head.

3 His purposes will ripen fast,
Unfolding ev'ry hour.
The bud may have a bitter taste,
But sweet will be the flow'r.

4 Blind unbelief is sure to err
And scan his work in vain.
God is his own interpreter,
And he will make it plain.

---

3 William Cowper, "God Moves in a Mysterious Way," https://hymnary.org/text/god_moves_in_a_mysterious_way.

Questions for Reflection

1. What is an example of someone giving you karmic advice about God's mysterious providences?

2. How could you encourage someone to persevere when they feel like God is mad at them for something they can't figure out?

3. What is one take-away from this chapter on God's purposes that you could share with someone to encourage them?

Chapter 2

Karma and Christian Assurance

Scripture for Memory
There is no fear in love, but perfect love casts out fear.
(1 John 4:18a)

Redemption Community Church hosted their annual father-son camp out in the mountains outside the city. The event was always designed to be a time of refreshment and reconnection for the generations of men in the church. Usually, they would plan activities such as fishing, hiking, bush-crafting, and devotions around the campfire.

Every night, as they roasted marshmallows or sipped hot chocolate, the guest speaker, Josh, tried to motivate the men to "radical obedience." His theme for the week was "Passing the Test," based on the book of 1 John. One night Josh gave a rousing summons to the men to spend their lives in total surrender. Nothing less than making Jesus Lord of their lives would suffice. He charged them to examine their obedience and test whether they were truly saved.

Josh gave some examples from his life of when he struggled with assurance of salvation. He never felt like he was good enough. He recalled when his start-up business was losing money faster than he could manage, his second year of marriage was spiraling out of control and on the brink of divorce, and his old sports injuries began revisiting him with chronic aches and pains. Three of the things he loved most in life—success, sex, and health—were all slipping out of his grip. So, he struggled with bitterness and doubt in his relationship to God. He grew up as a good Christian kid, but as his life unraveled, he knew something had to change. He had to change. God was trying to get his attention. There had to be a problem he could find so he could fix it.

Josh explained that his life fell apart because he had not made Jesus Lord of his life. He was a fan, not a follower. He made the case that faith without works is dead and that a true Christian pursues faithfulness, not faith (Jas 2:26). Faith is for new believers; faithfulness is for true believers. Pulling out his patriotic flair, Josh called the men to unbroken fealty and allegiance as the test they must pass to prove that they are true followers of Christ. He would repeat 1 John 2:3 over and over: "And by this we know that we have come to know him, if we keep his commandments." The condition for passing the test? Obedience. And the way to obey and the proof for assurance, Josh said, was found in 1 John 2:7–11—the test of love.

Josh pushed this point hard every night: "We can know that God loves us because we obey him by loving others." In other words, our assurance of salvation will grow as far as we grow in obedience to God by loving others. On top of that, once we have assurance of our salvation, if we obey God and love others even more, then we will experience more and more blessings.

Josh would then give the men hope by testifying to the power of obedience from his life. Once he hit rock bottom and doubted his salvation, he vowed to get serious with his obedience to God. As he labored to be kind to his estranged wife, slowly the joy in his marriage came back. They were now having the time of their life. And as for their intimacy? Sizzling. As he worked at customer satisfaction in his business, he was amazed at how God brought in more sales to the point that he sold his business and successfully started and sold five more businesses. All this since he got serious about following God. And, maybe the hardest of all, Josh learned to love himself. He focused more on self-care, eating healthy, sleeping better, and exercising more. Since then, much of his chronic pain had subsided and his body was looking more like a ripped thirty-something than a middle-aged man. He was on top of his game. The return on investment of obedience to God always pays. Josh was a living example of a loyal life that God blesses.

Scoring Your Own Test: "A" Is for Assurance?

As contrived as the above example may be, all Christians have struggled with assurance. In fact, all people, believers or unbelievers, battle feelings of insecurity and anxiety. It's not a Christian problem; it's a fallen human problem. Yet, no other ideologies, value systems, or cultural/religious beliefs provide a system that guarantees assurance. Some might imply degrees of assurance based upon devout adherence to some moral code or ritual, but only Christianity guarantees true assurance.

When Christians struggle with assurance, we typically assume that we need Scriptures to teach us how to live in a way that produces the feeling of assurance. And, as illustrated above, the book of 1 John is a classic text many have used as an "in-or-out" test for the Christian life. Unfortunately, so many Christians misunderstand how assurance works in 1 John. For most of my Christian life I read 1 John as listing conditions to follow obediently in order to derive a sense of assurance of salvation. Only in some good seasons did I actually feel assured of my salvation after reading 1 John. Usually, I felt anxious that I might be a fake Christian. Was I truly loving God with my whole heart? Could I really say I was loving those around me as much as I love myself? And if I answered, "yes," was I a liar? After all, John says, "Whoever says 'I know him' but does not keep his commandments is a liar, and the truth is not in him" (1 John 2:4).

So many of us misunderstand the purpose of 1 John when we tear some of the more unsettling verses out of context. John's whole purpose is to bring comfort to those who believe. He's not writing to rattle them into doubting their salvation or God's happiness with them if they aren't passing the test well enough.

We need to know the context of the epistle. Three groups of people were causing problems within the church: (1) those who believed that everything immaterial was good, so only spiritual realities mattered—anything done in the flesh was inconsequential; (2) those who believed that Jesus was merely Spirit that appeared to be fleshly; and (3) those who committed apostasy and left the church altogether. Those in the third group were the ones who were to be anxious about the state of their souls, not the saints. In light of the heartache and headache these deceived and false brethren were causing, John writes to give assurance to those who believe in Christ as God in the flesh who died for sins and rose from the dead. He explains his purpose is to comfort the saints: "I write these things to you who believe in the name of the Son of God, that you may know that you have eternal life" (1 John 5:13).

The aim of 1 John is to comfort the saints with the truth that God truly loves them. The saints should rest in the assuring doctrine of Christ. Christians grow in their assurance through studying the offices of Christ (Prophet, Priest, and King) and his power to forgive and justify. The duty of any competent teacher who rightly divides the word is to assure Christians in the faith and to lift up the external work of God on the cross. This teaching is key for true assurance because the external work of the triune God on Golgotha is finished. It is objective, outside of us, perfected for us. But if we look to internal workings of God in our lives, we will see only a process of change, in which we have a lifetime yet to grow. The sanctification process is subjective, inside of us, and not yet perfected. To put it another way: our assurance fundamentally rests in Christ's perfected work for us two thousand years ago, not Christ's perfecting work in us today. Our assurance of salvation is in the object of our faith, not the quality of our faithfulness. Our faithfulness is a necessary consequence of salvation, and we should rejoice when we see its necessary evidence, but our faithfulness is never a necessary condition of our salvation. Christ's faithfulness is the only necessary condition of our salvation. So, our assurance is in Christ and his work for us alone. Consider a small sample of the lavish confirmations and encouragements John gives to anxious saints:

- 1 John 2:12–14: "I am writing to you, little children, because your sins are forgiven for his name's sake. I am writing to you, fathers, because you know him who is from the beginning. I am writing to you, young men, because you have overcome the evil one. I write to you, children, because you know the Father. I write to you, fathers, because you know him who is from the beginning. I write to you, young men, because you are strong, and the word of God abides in you, and you have overcome the evil one."

- 1 John 2:21: "I write to you, not because you do not know the truth, but because you know it, and because no lie is of the truth."

- 1 John 3:1–2: "See what kind of love the Father has given to us, that we should be called children of God; and so we are. … Beloved, we are God's children now, and what we will be has not yet appeared; but we know that when he appears we shall be like him, because we shall see him as he is."

- 1 John 3:19–21: "By this we shall know that we are of the truth and reassure our heart before him; for whenever our heart condemns us, God is greater than our heart, and he knows everything. Beloved, if our heart does not condemn us, we have confidence before God."

- 1 John 4:9–10: "In this the love of God was made manifest among us, that God sent his only Son into the world, so that we might live through him. In this is love, not that we have loved God but that he loved us and sent his Son to be the propitiation for our sins."

Imperfect Love Creates Anxiety

John says that "there is no fear in love, but perfect love casts out fear" (1 John 4:18). That perfect love is not our love for God; it is God's love for us. And it is perfect, not partial. And that love is not merely some sentimental emotion God has for us depending on how well we are obeying and loving him in return. That love is rooted in a historical event with objective spiritual effects. God loved us first, when we were dead in our sins, and sent Christ to absorb God's wrath for our sins (1 John 4:10). Even more clearly, Paul says, "But God shows his love for us in that while we were still sinners, Christ died for us" (Rom 5:8). Do you want to know how God loves you? What must you do? Impress him? Praise him? Serve him? This verse says that God shows us, in the present tense, his love for us. So, today, God shows his love for us. But how? In what? By reminding us through the Spirit again and again that while we were dead in our sins, Christ died on a bloody Roman cross for us. The historical, objective truth of Christ's crucifixion for sinners is God telling you today that he loves you. That kind and quality of love should obliterate fear. It should flood your soul with peace and assurance. *God loves me!*

But, much of karmic Christianity comes from a defective understanding of God's love for us. We are motivated to grow in assurance because we are anxious. And if perfect love casts out fear, then conversely, imperfect love creates anxiety. Our tendency to try to do whatever we can to keep God happy with us reveals that we don't have assurance and peace in his love because our view of God's love is too small. Or, frankly, we think God loves the same as we love or have been loved.

If we are honest, all of us will readily admit that love is elusive. Billions of dollars are spent hyper-sexualizing love and marketing it as self-discovery and self-satisfaction. Anyone caught up in sexual addiction knows what is packaged as "true love" is instead true loss. It's a loss of what makes humans special in God's image—a dehumanizing of our selves. But on the other end of the spectrum of human love, even in the most moral, traditional, and well-ordered nuclear family where a warm spirit of love generally adorns the home, feelings of love and peace come and go. Even the best father is an imperfect father. Every family has an unwritten code. And only the compliant can enjoy its benefits. Even in the sweetest moments of familial solidarity where everyone is happy and full of laughter, the filial emotion fades. Even when men fight a raging battle or end an epic journey, the brotherly camaraderie dwindles. Even the dopamine surge of sexual intimacy diminishes.

All that the human experience calls "love" will never last. Even in its sublime moments when time seems to stop, love flashes across our consciousness like lightning in a dark sky—beautiful and gone. Like a vanishing sunset, the soul longs for love again. We could sense it but never truly know it. It awakens in us a desire for something otherworldly because nothing in this world can slake our thirst. And so, we project upon God imperfect love because our human point of reference is temporary, changeable, measurable, and conditional. Such imperfect love creates anxiety. Where love is mystifying, peace is a cryptic code to crack. And karma becomes our key to decoding the riddle.

What is Assurance?

We can indeed experience peace with God, but it is only experienced subjectively because it is a sure, solid, unchanging objective reality: "Therefore, since we have been justified by faith, we have peace with God through our Lord Jesus Christ" (Rom 5:1). Our present experience of peace is rooted in the unbreakable promise that we have been (at some time in the past with ongoing effects) justified through faith alone in Christ alone. But until we stop playing around with following the right rules, using the best methods, ensuring pure motives, and surrendering all in order to achieve a moment's rest in our hearts, we will languish in a karmic desert of never being good enough. We will wonder what we did to detract from God's pleasure, or we will wonder what we could do better to improve his pleasure. We end up temporarily assuring ourselves that though we don't have peace with God sometimes, surely, we will make it. And then we give in to temptation. We feel ashamed. We feel anxious. We get serious about obedience again. We recommit our lives and really mean it this time. The cycle reboots.

Assurance is not primarily a feeling that we have based upon our perception of our obedience. Assurance is fundamentally rooted in faith alone, in Christ alone. And faith requires knowledge, assent, and trust. We must know the teachings of Scripture about Christ: his humanity and divinity, his offices as Prophet, Priest, and King. We must also know the teachings of Scripture about Christ's redemptive work: his fulfilling the law for our righteousness, his satisfying the law for our atonement, his securing God's promises through his resurrection, and his applying God's blessings through his indwelling Spirit. We must assent and confess that these teachings are true. And we must personally trust in Christ and his work on our behalf.

In other words, we must know that the literal Jesus of Nazareth died on a cross and rose from the dead—that is history. We assent that Jesus, the God-Man, died for sins and was raised from the dead for sinners' justification— that is doctrine. We must also confess with our mouth and trust in our heart that this Jesus did all this in love for me, a sinner in need of mercy— that is gospel. Yet, knowledge and assent, though essential, are not saving faith. Even the demons know and assent to the history of the cross and the resurrection and to what the Bible teaches about Christ and his redemptive work. Believing like a demon is not saving faith.

Christ's gospel is the object of our assurance. And all we need for assurance is a hearty trust that receives and rests in Christ and his work for us. That's faith alone, or *sola fide*. Though not a model of stellar faithfulness, Abraham is certainly a model of faith alone. He was,

> Fully convinced that God was able to do what he had promised. That is why faith was "counted to him as righteousness." But the words "it was counted to him" were not written for his sake alone, but for ours also. It will be counted to us who believe in him who raised from the dead

Jesus our Lord, who was delivered up for our trespasses and raised for our justification. (Rom 4:21–25)

Our assurance is in Christ. Our assurance is in the God who keeps his promises, who swears to his own hurt and does not change. Our assurance is not mainly our joyful feelings. Not our loyal obedience. Not our extravagant praise. Those are the evidential fruits of the gospel's roots in our life, and we praise God for them. They enhance our enjoyment of our surety in Christ, but they do not replace the objective state of our assurance. They are not the ground of our assurance. The ground of our assurance is the full, free, and forever love of God in Christ for sinners. We can rest in peace, confident that God loves to save sinners. Consider this example:

[An] analogy might recreate a conversation of three Hebrews in Egypt milling around outside their houses a few hours before the Passover. One man, anxious to his bones, sheepishly asks his neighbor, "So are you worried at all about Yahweh striking down all the firstborn tonight?" His neighbor responds, "No way! I'm absolutely certain God will get us through this. I have not a worry in the world." And his second neighbor chortles softly, "I don't think much about it. All I know is that we're supposed to put the blood of an unblemished, male, year-old lamb on our house's doorposts."

After discussing what they know has been commanded, they all agree to put blood on their houses and go inside and rest till morning. And after Yahweh slays all the firstborn in Egypt that night, of the three Hebrew neighbors, whose household was hit the hardest? The anxious man with little faith? The confident man with illustrious faith? Or the shallow man with relaxed faith? The answer is, none of them. Their salvation depends exclusively on the efficacy of the lamb's blood and the faithfulness of Yahweh's promise. Was the lamb's blood on each house sufficient for Yahweh to pass over? Yes. Is Yahweh faithful to his word? Yes. Each man knew the promise, agreed it was true, and rested under the blood of the lamb. That's *sola fide*. Simple. We do not boast in our faith plus our ability to know anything, obey anything, or experience anything. Anything in addition is not Christianity. Our boast is in the blood.[1]

---

1 E. D. Burns, *Seeds and Stars: Resting in Christ for Great Commission Service* (Cape Coral, FL: Founders Press, 2023), 121. I'm grateful to Dr. Don Carson for first sharing a similar analogy in a lecture I heard years ago. I have since adapted it for my own illustrations.

Assurance Drives Christian Life, Growth, and Service

As we will see in the following chapters, how we understand our assurance before God directly influences how we perceive our Christian living, our role in Christian growth and its outcome in our lives, and our role in Christian service and its outcome in the lives of others. The importance of getting the biblical doctrine of assurance right cannot be overstated. Understanding the ground of our assurance is absolutely essential for growing in grace and serving by the Spirit. If we get the ground of our assurance wrong and confuse it with good feelings or good works, our daily experiences, discipleship, spiritual growth practices, and outreach efforts will all be mixed with error, works righteousness, and a false notion of karmic Christianity. Our motivations and methods in Christian growth and service are indexes for how we conceive the basis of our assurance before God.

Ballast in Our Boat

Revisiting the illustration at the beginning of this chapter, we have probably all interpreted changes in life like Josh explained. In one season it seems like life couldn't get any worse, but it's for no noticeable corresponding sin. So we try to decipher what God might be teaching us. After all, there is a lesson here that we want to learn so we don't have to go through this again. If we just learn the rules and play our cards right, we'll win and not lose next time. And then when the season changes and good times are on the horizon, we rejoice that we passed the test. Our obedience and strong faith got us through. God was pleased enough to tip the scales now in our favor. So, when we sing praises to him with hands stretched high and feel the surge of emotion, we are assured that God is happy with us. If we're happy in God, it must mean he's happy with us. Though an emotional release might be intense and ecstatic, it's not the basis for our assurance. As a trained musician, I love singing with passion and deep-seated affection for God. Somber music that lacks dynamic volume and beautiful chord progressions seems unfitting for Christ-centered praise. The best is when our affections and the glorious truths we affirm rise together. I praise God for joyful feelings, to be sure. They are God-given moments for us to enjoy. But I must remind myself even in those emotive moments of hearty praise that our security and peace are united to God alone. Not our feelings. Not the musical dynamic changes.

God shows us his love every day by reminding us of the bloody cross, empty tomb, and all the attached promises that are yes and amen in Christ. We rejoice in hope of the glory of God. This hope is ours to enjoy in part now as we look to the cross and hope in the promises God secured for believers. The love of God is poured out into our hearts by the Holy Spirit through trust alone in the word of Christ. This is the ballast in our boat when the waves of the curse, sin, and the devil beat upon our souls. Jesus is the helmsman in the storm. He will deliver us to our heavenly home when the morning dawns at the edge of the sea. He who called you is faithful. He will surely do it (1 Thess 5:24).

Hymn for Reflection

"My Hope Is Built on Nothing Less"[2]

1 My hope is built on nothing less
than Jesus' blood and righteousness;
I dare not trust the sweetest frame,
but wholly lean on Jesus' name.

Refrain:
On Christ, the solid Rock, I stand:
all other ground is sinking sand;
all other ground is sinking sand.

2 When darkness veils his lovely face,
I rest on his unchanging grace;
in every high and stormy gale,
my anchor holds within the veil. [Refrain]

---

2 Edward Mote, "My Hope Is Built on Nothing Less," https://hymnary.org/text/my_hope_is_built_on_nothing_less.

3 His oath, his covenant, his blood,
support me in the whelming flood;
when all around my soul gives way,
he then is all my hope and stay. [Refrain]

4 When he shall come with trumpet sound,
O may I then in him be found:
dressed in his righteousness alone,
faultless to stand before the throne. [Refrain]

Questions for Reflection

1. How have you understood assurance for much of your Christian life?

2. When you think of discipleship and spiritual growth, how does assurance affect what you do?

3. What is one take-away from this chapter on assurance that you could share with someone to encourage them?

Chapter 3

Karma and Christian Living

Scripture for Memory
*I have been crucified with Christ. It is no longer I who live,
but Christ who lives in me. And the life I now live in the flesh
I live by faith in the Son of God, who loved me and gave
himself for me.* (Gal 2:20)

Anna left her small-town Baptist roots after high school and moved to the
big city to work in a coffee shop. One of her coworkers always seemed so
upbeat and sincere. She was always talking about her church. One Friday
Anna joined her coworker for a late-night prayer event with some twenty-
somethings from the church. Anna was startled by how disorderly it
seemed—everyone praying aloud at the top of their lungs, the worship leaders
singing repetitive choruses that they seemed to make up as they sang, and
no teaching at all unless you counted the prophetic utterances from a young
lady on the keyboard (usually about someone needing healing or something
vague about angels and demons in the city) interjected between choruses.
The more Anna went back with her friend, the more she felt hooked by
the passion, enthusiasm, and overwhelming emotional release that would
cascade with the musical dynamic changes.

Eventually, Anna enrolled as an intern at the church to train intercessors
and worship leaders. She attended a conference where she first tasted the
glory. "That conference was on fire! The worship was so anointed." Anna
relayed to her friend, "We called down the Spirit." She would go from there
to learn about soaking prayer, dream interpretation, prophetic singing, and

binding generational curses. The more she pressed into the Spirit and sang with reckless abandon, the more the anointing flowed into her life. The more she had emotional confidence that God's presence was with her, the more she could claim his promises by faith.

Caleb grew up in a small family-oriented house church away from the compromising effects of society. The church gathered weekly in someone's home for a meal, prayer, and teaching. The church consisted of four families, and all the men were considered elders. They were the authorities, and they watched over the souls of all the women and children. They would often counsel Caleb, "If you want to walk in the Lord's blessing, you must walk with the wise." The fathers of the church would oversee the spending habits, the entertainment choices, the devotional practices, and even the frequency and satisfaction of intimacy between couples.

Once Caleb came of age, he was instructed by the men in the church to get a job working for one of the men, find a wife, and have a lot of children. To get his job certification, Caleb had to move to an adjacent city for training. While living alone, he would read his Bible vigorously, revisit many of the notes he took from the wisdom of his elders, and pray without doubting. He knew that God would only hear his prayers if he didn't regard iniquity in his heart. Caleb was devastated, though, when we didn't pass his first certification exam. What had he done so wrong that God would abandon him? Was it because he cut short his devotions a few mornings to get ready for classes? Was it because he entertained some lustful thoughts too long in his head when he saw some pretty girls at the vocational school? Was it because he spent outside his prescribed food budget? Was it because he failed to believe without doubting when he prayed? Was he double-minded, professing one thing in his prayers but lacking enough faith? How could he have walked away from the Lord's presence? How could he get back?

The above anecdotes of Anna and Caleb are probably more extreme than the average evangelical Christian might experience. But they indeed capture a spectrum of karmic Christianity as it's applied to Christian living. On one side of the spectrum, there is the victorious Christian life, moving from one anointed spiritual buzz to another. The experience of inexpressible joy rises as the Christian claims God's blessings and calls down the fire. On the other side of the spectrum, there is the dutiful Christian life, passing one test at a time, proving the effectiveness of a righteous life of pure motives and check-list-obedience. The experience of spiritual success rises as the Christian follows the rules, guards their heart, and stays unstained by the world. On the spectrum between these two extremes are variations of many other karmic formulas for Christian growth and spiritual success. Not all are as rigid and cult-like, but every karmic view of the Christian life is equally insidious and treacherous to the soul. People on this spectrum are generally quite serious about walking with the Lord and doing their best, to their credit. But another common aspect is that these driven Christians are often exhausted and unsettled. They are not sure that they're doing enough, believing enough, loving enough, and praying enough. Since they can't know, they try harder. They try different ideas and techniques. They never want to settle for second best, which is actually code for feeling anxious. No stable assurance. No enduring peace.

What about Blessings for Piety and Obedience?

The Bible teaches that God will bless obedience. There is no debate there. The problem arises when we over apply or misapply passages of proverbial wisdom and turn potentials into promises. In other words, we must be careful not to reinvent wisdom principles as success formulas. For instance, it is not uncommon to hear someone quote Proverbs 22:6, "Train up a child in the way he should go; even when he is old he will not depart from it," as an assertion that if parents use a certain variety of parenting techniques, the child is guaranteed to grow up to be successful, godly, mature, and an example of the parenting that God blesses. To be sure, there is proverbial wisdom to training up children in righteousness as opposed to letting children follow their sinful impulses. The generational consequences can be devastating for ill-trained children. But when the wisdom principles turn into success formulas they become rigid techniques with measurable outcomes: "If you do ____ enough, then you can expect _____."

The story of Jacob and Esau essentially blows this view out of the water. God chose Jacob before birth for special purposes, in spite of Jacob's deceptive tendencies and wrestling with God. Yet God also blessed Esau through much rebellion and struggle. But the unique purposes of God were not fulfilled in Esau as they were in Jacob. Jacob didn't deserve the Messianic blessings and salvation more than Esau. The Bible interprets this event by putting the condition of blessing upon the promise giver of the blessing:

> It is not the children of the flesh who are the children of God, but the children of the promise are counted as offspring. For this is what the promise said: "About this time next year I will return, and Sarah shall have a son." And not only so, but also when Rebekah had conceived children by one man, our forefather Isaac, though they were not yet born and had done nothing either good or bad—in order that God's purpose of election might continue, not because of work but because of him who calls—she was told, "The older will serve the younger." As it is written, "Jacob I loved, but Esau I hated." What shall we say then? Is there injustice on God's part? By no means! For he says to Moses, "I will have mercy on whom I have mercy, and I will have compassion on whom I have compassion." So then it depends not on human will or exertion, but on God, who has mercy. (Rom 9:8–16)

We would do well to remind ourselves that the true blessings of God are eternal salvation blessings that flow from his sovereign purposes to save people for Christ from before the foundation of the world:

> Blessed be the God and Father of our Lord Jesus Christ, who has blessed us in Christ with every spiritual blessing in the heavenly places, even as he chose us in him before the foundation of the world, that we should be holy and blameless before him. In love he predestined us for adoption to himself as sons through Jesus Christ, according to the purpose of his will, to the praise of his glorious grace, with which he has blessed us in the Beloved. (Eph 1:3–6)

Karmic Interpretations of God's Historical Providences

It is true that in God's common grace, he causes it to rain on the just and the unjust. And there are generally good results and kind blessings from the Lord for those people in all cultures and epochs who abide by the natural law of God on their hearts. They may not be regenerate believers in Christ, but by abiding by the moral law on their hearts, they can enjoy temporal provisions of stability, civility, and pleasure in life. This reality is part of God's grace that he gives to humankind in spite of our hard-hearted rebellion. But if God chooses to inordinately bless a nation more than another, it is not necessarily evidence that such a nation is favored or especially moral. It could be that God has unique purposes for a particular nation for a particular season. After all, God alone builds up nations and tears them down (Dan 2:21), and he alone steers the hearts of kings as a watercourse (Prov 21:1).

For these reasons, we need to reject the sentiment that God blesses nations to the degree that the churches in those nations are obedient and successfully promote righteousness. This notion has been quite common when people positively say, "God has blessed America because she was founded on Christian principles." But this response is not an American phenomenon. Christians in other countries and eras have maintained similar assessments when their nations were at the height of imperial power—Great Britain, Germany, France, and Spain, among others. It's also not uncommon to hear countries in contemporary Africa, Asia, and Latin America express the same notion that if the national church were more faithful and prayerful, then God would bless their nation with greater economic growth, social justice, abundance of temporal comforts, and overall human and cultural flourishing.

However, this belief implies that nations where corruption and poverty-related diseases run rampant must not have enough Christians, or those Christians are dysfunctional, disobedient, and divided. If only Christians in a nation would unite, pray, align themselves in total surrender, and commit all their ways to the Lord, then he would heal their land and bless their nation with the dew of heaven. So, then, what about those nations where Christians are persecuted and martyred without mercy? Where their suffering, poverty, and persecution are not short seasons? Their pain goes on and on for generations without relief. What about them? According to the above karmic system of blessing, the implication then is that these Christians are not faithful and obedient enough because God has not blessed them like he has their healthy and wealthy counterparts in other countries. Has God blessed the American church more than the Sudanese church? Was Nazi Germany God's punishment upon a lukewarm German church, or the Reign of Terror God's punishment on a feeble French church? Does the totalitarian regime of China imply that the persecuted believers are not obedient and faith-filled enough to merit God's national blessing? Why would God, then, permit temporal blessings of health and wealth in Western nations that defy God's created order and celebrate all manner of sexual perversion and dysphoria? As Billy Graham would commonly say, "If God doesn't judge America, he'll need to apologize to Sodom and Gomorrah." By logical and historical observation, the karmic system of obedience and blessing doesn't work out the way it should.

Could it be that we have become theologically sloppy with our vocabulary of "blessing"?

Instead of speaking of God blessing the church in America in the twentieth century or the English church in the nineteenth century (and by implication passing over the church in Cambodia or the church in Algeria), we should remember that all the blessings for God's people are promised in total in the resurrection. We do not merit or improve God's blessings in this life based upon a karmic form of contractual obedience. It might be that God is pleased to give temporal blessings to some in this life more than others, but these blessings are not payouts for enough faithfulness or even rewards for sufficient, prayerful faith. We should view them more as unique responsibilities and opportunities to honor God and take the gospel to the least-reached. The temporal blessings of God are for the sake of his kingdom. We should interpret them as designed for the Great Commission, not as echoes of our hard work and sufficient piety for us to enjoy for ourselves. The mysterious providences of kindness are ours to use responsibly while we have opportunity. They are not for self-indulgence or self-congratulation.

Some Christians are graced with the responsibility and opportunity of health, wealth, and freedom to travel and broadcast the gospel. Other Christians are graced with the responsibility and opportunity of suffering, persecution, and martyrdom to testify to the gospel. Healthy, wealthy, and free Christians are no more blessed in Christ than the sick, poor, and imprisoned Christians. We all inherit the same blessings together in the resurrection. Some are triumphant by faith, while others are tortured by faith. Our Good Shepherd leads some to pasture beside still water, while he leads others through the raging rivers to the slaughter. Whether he handles us with tenderness or hands us over to torture, faith says, "Jesus is my inheritance."

Consider how Jesus answers Peter at the end of John's Gospel about Peter's curiosity as to why he would suffer for Christ while John would die of old age:

"Truly, truly, I say to you, when you were young, you used to dress yourself and walk wherever you wanted, but when you are old, you will stretch out your hands, and another will dress you and carry you where you do not want to go." (This he said to show by what kind of death he was to glorify God.) And after saying this he said to him, "Follow me." Peter turned and saw the disciple whom Jesus loved following them ... When Peter saw him, he said to Jesus, "Lord, what about this man?" Jesus said to him, "If it is my will that he remain until I come, what is that to you? You follow me!" So the saying spread abroad among the brothers that this disciple was not to die; yet Jesus did not say to him that he was not to die, but, "If it is my will that he remain until I come, what is that to you?" (John 21:18–23)

Whether we suffer and die a terrible death or live long and enjoy sweetness with Christ all our days, the purpose is the same: that we would glorify God. Our job is to not untangle the reasons why some of God's children suffer while others seem to go from one victory to another. That's up to God to know and us to silently trust. We must only follow Christ.

Sinai Versus Zion

Towering across the pages of Scripture and truly across human history are two metaphorical mountains. They represent two groups of people. They are Sinai and Zion. Sinai represents what is natural to all of us, not just the Jews. Sinai is a summary of laws that are part of the moral law written on the hearts of all humans. All persons and all societies operate according to a moral rudder of love for neighbor and justice for the evildoer. Without this common moral code, the civic order would devolve into chaos and anarchy. Sinai is what orders families, societies, and history. What is the cost of order, progress, and overall human flourishing? Obedience. Faithfulness. Following the rules.

Zion represents what is supernatural—grace and salvation through sacrifice. Not surprisingly, many myths and beloved legends in most cultures throughout history have told tales of the highest virtue. What is that common myth that every culture loves to tell? It can be summed up as the story of love that saves through sacrifice. Or, love that lays down its life for its friends (John 15:13). This story is embedded in our blockbuster movies that make us cry and in those heart-warming legends that cultures love to tell their children to shape their virtues.

Though these stories are typically fairytales and fantasies, there is one real story that makes sense of them all. It is the truest of true myths. It is the lore of Zion. It is the story of a benevolent Sovereign who lays down his life for his enemies at the hand of his enemies. He makes this sacrifice to reconcile them to himself and make them into a kingdom of priests to dwell with him as his co-heirs. What is the cost of entrance into this heavenly inheritance and abundant peace and happiness? It's the same as the cost for Sinai—obedience, faithfulness, and following the rules. But the better question is, "Who can pay the bill?" The King of Zion paid it all with his life. So now, through trust alone in him alone, his enemies can be declared justified citizens, adopted into his royal family. He pays the bill and we get the blessings. The kingdom is ours to receive, not achieve. With a hearty trust, we can rest assured that his promises are unconditionally ours to enjoy, based upon the condition of his unbreakable faithfulness to the honor of his name.

To achieve the potential benefits of the law covenant, we must be spotless and blameless. All we must do is work for his approval. And the people say, "Look at all we have done for you." However, to receive the promised blessings of Zion, the King descended the mount spotless and blameless. All we must do is rest in his approval. And the people say, "Look at all he has done for us." Sinai says, "Do all this and you shall live." Zion says, "All this he has done so that you shall live."

The battle for the believer is to rest secure in Zion. Our old slavery to Sinai's stipulations clings so tightly. We are wired to seek God's approval and blessing based upon our performance. The promises of God in Christ are sure, and we will receive them in the resurrection. But in our old Sinai mindset, we live like the promises are potentials that Christ made possible for us to achieve in this life if we are good enough.

Sinai and Another Gospel

Paul battles the tendency to confuse Sinai and Zion in his letter to the Galatians. Some were arguing that the blessings promised to Abraham were based upon the condition of Moses's laws. Some believed they could get saved by faith but stay saved by faithfulness. They viewed salvation as getting in by justification through faith, and then staying in by sanctification through faith and works. But that is not the promise of the gospel. It is not merely an appointment for weak people to see a therapist, after which they do most of the work at home. No. The gospel is a heart transplant for dead people. It is blood transfusions and ongoing care. They contribute nothing other than trusting in the doctor's sufficient ability and honorable reputation. The Galatians were living out of sync with the promises of the gospel. They were living according to the rules given to Moses as though they were seeking to achieve the blessings of the earthly Jerusalem. But Paul called them to rest according to the promises given to Abraham because they were going to receive the blessings of the heavenly Jerusalem (Gal 3:7–21; 4:21–31).

Paul addressed a vast range of problems in all his epistles, even some of the most decadent and defiling sins in Corinth, but no issue alarms him more than this issue in Galatia. He says their conduct is not in step with the gospel (Gal 2:14). It's not that they were practicing defiling sexual sins or following prosperity preachers like those in Corinth. No, the Galatians were merely adding rule-keeping to the gospel to get its blessings. It appeared to be very pious and well-intentioned. After all, they were just trying to live the gospel, what's the big deal? Even Peter and Barnabas were deceived by this seemingly virtuous approach to adding good works to good news. Yet, after being publicly shamed, Peter and Barnabas repented and changed their teaching (Gal 2:11–14).

The combining of law and gospel for obtaining the promises exasperates Paul. Galatians is by far Paul's most heated letter. He even calls them "foolish" and "bewitched" (3:1), suggesting that this confusion of law and gospel is not merely a theological oversight. It is the work of the enemy. It is evidence of spiritual warfare, that truth terrorists have poisoned the fresh supply of gospel food. It might taste healthy, but if it is not thrown out, it will kill them. Paul says, anyone who is teaching another gospel like this should be thrown in hell (Gal 1:6–9), though of course, there's room to repent as Peter and Barnabas did. But that's how serious this issue is. It is not a wordsmith game of nuance and emphasis. As the Reformation taught, either you follow the standards perfectly that inherit the promised blessings of God, or you suffer the penalty for falling short of the standards that incur the curses of God (Gal 3:10–14).

Welcome to Sinai. Karmic Christianity is just Sinai in the disguise of good intentions and virtuous piety adding on to grace as though the promises were potentials for us to meet. In layman's terms, this is the difference between viewing the gospel as good advice versus a good announcement.

It is the difference between viewing the gospel as a subjective work internally renovating us versus an objective work externally redeeming us. It is the difference of Christ at work *in* us through our faithfulness versus Christ at work *for* us through our faith alone. Sinai views the gospel as the renewal of the soul, happening over time in light of our ability and willingness. Zion views the gospel as the redemption of the sinner, happening in three hours on a bloody Roman cross on Passover in Jerusalem in spite of our inability and unwillingness. Sinai says Jesus is our assistant who gives us aid if only we have enough faith and obedience. Zion says Jesus is our advocate who gives us acquittal if only we have faith alone in his obedience alone. The former is medieval Roman Catholic doctrine, and the latter is the ancient gospel of the apostles and the church fathers that the Reformation rediscovered. There's no third way. The Roman Catholic middle road—adding your effort to God's gracious assistance—is the pervasive notion throughout evangelicalism today. You don't partner with God's grace to make you acceptable enough to feel assured of his approval. The very doctrine of assurance in Christ alone by grace alone through faith alone slays karmic Christianity. The evangelical global church languishes under a kind of medieval spell that is functionally karma. It is driven by fear of not feeling, believing, thinking, and doing enough to keep God's blessings flowing. This is another gospel that the devil loves to propagate. He tricks us with employing the virtuous-sounding vocabulary of Sinai. For the citizens of Zion, our banner should be: "I have been crucified with Christ. It is no longer I who live, but Christ who lives in me. And the life I now live in the flesh I live by faith in the Son of God, who loved me and gave himself for me" (Gal 2:20).

Rest in Zion

The Christian life is neither one of carefree inaction nor fear-driven effort. Pushing back against karmic applications of Christian obedience should not encourage laziness or lukewarmess. Rather, a rightly ordered obedience to God's ways should grow out of gratitude and a joy in God's love in Christ's gospel. Because Christ is our guilt offering, we can come into God's presence with thanksgiving. The blessings of Zion encourage our spirits to rest secure in God's love. We can never improve upon his love or detract from it based upon our performance. From such an assured peace in God, we can follow him with glad-hearted contentment, knowing that all our righteousness is in heaven, seated at the right hand of God. And all the spiritual blessings and promises of God are secured for us in our union with Christ. Let God's blessings from Zion fill you with hope and joy inexpressible. May you live your life through faith in Christ who lives in you, and is your hope of glory.

Hymn for Reflection

"By Grace Alone"[1]

1 Out of the depths I cry to Thee,
Lord, hear my voice of pleading;
Bend down Thy gracious ear, I pray,
Thy humble servant heeding.
If Thou remember each misdeed,
And of each thought and word take heed,
Who shall abide Thy presence?

2 Thy pardon is a gift of love,
Thy grace alone must save us,
Our works will not our guilt remove,
The strictest life would fail us.
Let none in their own merits boast,
But let us own the Holy Ghost
Alone can make us righteous.

---

1 Martin Luther, translated by Catherine Winkworth, "By Grace Alone," https://www.christianhymnbook.com/hymn/out-of-the-depths-i-cry-to-thee-n-130-v-1.

3 Though great our sins and sore our woes
His grace much more aboundeth;
His helping love no limit knows,
Our utmost need it soundeth.
Our kind and faithful Shepherd He,
Who shall set all His people free
From all their sin and sorrow.

Questions for Reflection

1. Considering the analogies of Anna and Caleb, in what ways have you experienced some sort of karmic Christian living in your denomination or tradition?

2. How did the discussion of Sinai and Zion help clarify how Christians should understand receiving the promises of God?

3. What is one take-away from this chapter on assurance that you could share with someone to encourage them?

Chapter 4

Karma and Christian Growth

"Who was your favorite prof?" Liam asked his two roommates after their first semester of Bible college. Liam, Eric, and Brandon were going out for a Sunday night dinner on the eve of finals week. As they reflected on their experiences and tremendous spiritual growth, they each found themselves latching on to a particular professor who impacted them more than others.

Eric said, "My favorite professor was Dr. Agarwal. His Old Testament survey class was always so practical. I never really understood the OT before taking him. He made it come to life in a way that I finally understood how to teach and obey the God's commands. Every class would be filled with practical steps for walking with the Lord. It's amazing how Israel fell short so often. If they only had understood how to better obey God's word, I wonder if they would have been more successful as God promised Joshua."

Brandon responded, "The best class I had was Bible Backgrounds and Culture with Dr. Watkins. That guy knows his material. He pulled stuff out of the Bible, the worldviews of the Ancient Near East, and obscure sources that completely changed how I understood the message of the Bible. I always understood it as a message of Christ's redemption for sinners as we hope in heaven. But now I see it as a message of God's plan to transform the cosmos through the mission of his people. Jesus died for the cosmos, not just souls.

All this time I thought it was about what God did to save our souls, but now I understand it as what I get to do with God to change the world."

Liam then chimed in, "Honestly, I felt the love of God so much in the Spiritual Formation class with Dr. Yong. That was the best class. The way he prayed and invited the Spirit during class would give me chills. God's presence weighed heavily on us every Monday morning. He is so anointed. I am so glad that I took his class in my first semester. I think I would have lost my first love for Jesus by second semester without learning how to walk in the fullness of God's presence and learning to hear his voice."

Never Enough

We all tend to admire and emulate influential people in our lives that seem to arrive at great heights of spiritual success. How we each define spiritual success might be different, but we all look for keys and clues into the secret counsel of God. We listen for his secret words. We look for his secret will. And we long for his secret ways. We instinctively operate like there is a code to crack. God doles out secret blessings to the most persistent and faith-filled seekers. Some aspire to learn from the scholars, others wish to follow their sages, and others try to imbibe the cocktails of the spiritualists. They are all karmic consultants who inadvertently peddle their encryption codes. But those codes are not open-source material. They come at the price of doing, feeling, thinking, or believing something enough. That's the skeleton key that opens every lock: *enoughness*.

Consequently, the question is, *how* do you know when enough is enough? Apparently, it is when the perceived blessings of God outweigh the balance of the perceived punishments of God. But for the hyper-sensitive conscience, the question lingers: *what* must I do enough to be enough? Why does that Christian seem to walk in the fullness of blessing when I am doing my best and struggle day after day? The answer usually comes down to mastering a degree of either moral steps, esoteric speculation, or mystical experience. Yet, the Bible will not permit the karmic codes to stand: "None is righteous, no not one; no one understands; no one seeks for God" (Rom 3:10–11). There is no one perpetually and perfectly righteous: moralism falls short. There is no one who secretly and sufficiently understands: speculation falls short. There is no one who successfully seeks and secures the unmediated presence of God: mysticism falls short.

This does not mean that in light of natural law no one does anything good, no one knows anything, and no one actually seeks for the Creator. The problem is that no fallen person or fallen cultural value system effectively seeks God, truly understands God, and perfectly obeys God. Many people indeed try to the best of their ability in their fallen state, but that's the issue: they always fall short. No one successfully achieves the blessings of God through moralism, speculation, or mysticism. And God never gives a pass based upon sincere intentions. It's a pass/fail grade. Everyone fails.

The Way, the Truth, and the Life

For those who have gone to a fair or a circus and walked through a hall of mirrors, they might remember the feeling of being stuck in the maze of mirrors. Every direction they look, they see reflections of themselves bouncing off other mirrors. And some mirrors bend their image to look extra wide or extra tall. For a child stuck in the maze of mirrors, it can actually be terrifying because reality feels lost. The only normal thing they feel is the ground they stand upon. Once the child finds the exit out of the maze of mirrors, they are relieved not to be tormented by warped, ugly distortions of themselves. The security of being safe with their parents is incredibly peace-giving.

We are living in a maze of mirrors, and Jesus brings peace to our relentless pursuit of enoughness—obeying moral ways enough, learning truth enough, and seeking life enough. Jesus brings peace to the fearful realization that all our efforts are never enough. He is the solution to our problem: "I am the way, and the truth, and the life. No one comes to the Father except through me" (John 14:6).

Jesus is the Priest whose obedience in life and in death accomplished what moralism seeks to achieve: "I am the way." The way to the Father is found through faith alone in Christ alone.

Jesus is the Prophet that reveals in his word what speculation claims to retrieve: "I am the truth." We learn to know the Father through faith alone in Christ alone.

Jesus is the King who has authority to guarantee the fullness of life in the resurrection that mysticism seeks to experience now: "I am the life." We rejoice in hope of the glory of God the Father through faith alone in Christ alone.

Faith Alone and Karmic Distortions

These karmic distortions of the way to the Father, the truth of the Father, and the life in the Father threaten the essential nature of faith alone. Faith alone requires three things: knowledge, assent, and trust. We must know the truth of Christ and his work, which is history. Yet, secular historians can know this. We must assent that the truth of Christ and his work is indeed true and affects our eternity, which is doctrine. Yet, demons can assent to this. Finally we must personally trust the truth of Christ and his work for us, which is gospel. Only Christians can trust this. The battle for Christian growth is to remember that one feeble thread of true faith alone in Christ alone is more pleasing to God than a life of our best obedience apart from faith. This truth applies even to those with the purest motives and the most wholehearted love for God and neighbor. A frail arm of true faith alone in one moment receives an eternity of all Christ's righteousness and promised blessings, while ten thousand strong arms of faithfulness fail to achieve one millisecond of righteousness and blessing.

These karmic counterfeits attack faith alone by offering alternatives for coming to the Father through the way of Christ as Priest, the truth of Christ as Prophet, and the life of Christ as King. Faith alone is the very heart of our instrumental connection to God's promised blessings. These counterfeits add to or subtract from the simplicity of resting alone in Christ alone and receiving promised blessings of God.

Speculation boasts of special knowledge—a sin of the mind. It commands, "Know more!" And the haunting question is, "Do I know enough?" Yet our Prophet reveals true wisdom and knowledge in his gospel.

Moralism assents to the sufficiency of its rule-keeping—a sin of the will. It demands, "Do more and do better!" And the haunting question is, "Have I done enough?" Yet our Priest shows the way through his finished work.

Mysticism trusts in its ability to seek and secure unmediated intimate communion with God—a sin of the heart. It promises, "You can ascend!"

And the haunting question is, "Have I sought God enough?" Yet our King condescended to fulfill the promises and then has ascended back to his holy mountain where he prepares a place of joy inexpressible in his Father's house.

Faith in Faith?

Another possible distortion of faith alone is faith in faith. This is where we confuse the object of our faith (Christ) with faith itself. You can hear it when we cope with mysteriously severe providences and say something like, "The only thing that got me through was my faith," "I just had to believe," and "I have strong faith." This kind of "faith" is code for psychological certainty, which we can manufacture with concentrated prayer until we feel content with our efforts. Finally, we worked up enough "faith" to lift the unsettled angst. We are no longer anxious about the prayed-for situation; we now have a psychological sense of relief and emotional release. We call it "inner peace." The "check in our spirit" has diminished. We've had enough faith to move mountains. Our faith has released the angelic hosts in the heavenlies to push back the powers of darkness that prevent us from laying hold of all of God's blessings for us.

Nevertheless, if we didn't have enough faith, then God's blessings would sadly sit in heaven waiting for us to work up faith the size of a mustard seed. How pathetic we must seem to God that we can't even get our act together and believe enough. If we're honest, we don't really know when we have increased our faith to mustard-seed size, but that warm feeling of psychological release is our cue that we have reestablished peace with God through enough faith. We prayed intensely enough. We sang with extravagant love enough. We surrendered all and we meant it enough. We let go and let God enough. We submitted blindly to our spiritual authorities in every way enough. We studied and learned enough. And in light of our assurance of enoughness, we have observed some signs of God's approval. The signs are a bit nebulous, but we reassure ourselves that our strong faith connection to God is just being attacked by the enemy. That's a good sign that we are still in God's will and walking in his Spirit. Spiritual warfare is a sign that we are over the target. That must mean our faith is strong enough. Good things are on their way. Let the good times roll.

This kind of faith in faith is like a passenger on an airplane whose small son is afraid of flying. What if the parent reassures their son that he should trust in his ability to sit still and buckle up for the whole flight, and that will get him to his destination? The child might buy it for a little while, but what happens when he needs to go to the toilet? Assurance is gone. So, he stands in the aisle, waiting his turn to go to the toilet, and he weakens in his assurance that he's going to make it to his destination. And then what if there is bad turbulence while he's in the aisle? Might the child then interpret it as happening because he's not buckled up? Instead, it would be better to transfer the son's trust away from anything he must do and remind him of the reliability and sufficiency of the pilot and the aircraft to deliver them to their destination safely. The son can rest assured up in the sky in his seat or in the lavatory as he receives the blessing of human flight. The pilot and his aircraft will deliver as promised.

Faith in Faithfulness?

The other distorted version of faith alone is faith in faithfulness. This is increasingly popular in some evangelical literature. This distortion is more easily measurable than faith in faith. This approach says that God blesses those whose obedience and repentance are enough. The riddle, as Job's friends might propose, is that if you are consistently struggling, then that means you have not added to faith commensurate faithfulness. But if you are being blessed, then that is the sign that you have solved the math equation:

- Faith – Enough Faithfulness = Random Painful Lessons
- Little Faith – Faithfulness = Patterns of Punishment
- Enough Faith + Enough Faithfulness = General Patterns of Blessing
- Strong Faith + Extraordinary Faithfulness = Amazing Outpourings of Blessing

To revisit the analogy above, faith in faithfulness would be like parents on a flight assuring their anxious son that they will get to their destination because they are loyal customers of that airline company. They never fly with any other airline. They will even spend extra above and beyond what the competitors charge just to fly that particular airline. And their loyalty is obvious—they got to board the flight first, and they were bumped to first class. Apparently, their customer loyalty shows signs of paying off. Surely they will get to their destination safely. After all, that's what they have been paying for all these years. The kickbacks from their loyalty is only growing, and so should their assurance. The son should wear his airlines sticker and tell himself that they are MVP frequent flyers. Everything should work in their favor.

Faith without faithfulness is dead. We don't want to love God and others in word and not in deed. More than that, if we really want to tap into God's reserves, we should seek to go beyond the baseline of obedience. Why not strive to be God's MVP, his favorite child, his teacher's pet? Doesn't the Bible say that God also desires sacrifice, not just obedience? Surely God is pleased to reward those whose hearts are truly his. This calls for reckless abandon, extravagant devotion, and radical discipleship. There are those who have enough faith and enough faithfulness to keep God happy with them and generally bless their spiritual growth, but then there are those who have added to their strong faith a level of otherworldly faithfulness that deserves hagiography. These saints pursue justice, imitate the ways of Jesus, pray without ceasing, hear Jesus calling, seek to redeem the culture, do their devotions daily, get busy at church, sit up front at all the gospel-centered conferences, and wait patiently for an inner prompting lest they make a decision out of step with the Spirit. Frankly, this is just a plain vanilla, straight laced, evangelical version of the prosperity gospel. It's good-old-boy, easy-listening, karmic Christianity.

Infusion or Imputation?

The approach to faithfulness in addition to faith is a rehash of the medieval Roman Catholic model of Christ's infused righteousness. The infused righteousness view said that Christ's gospel internally renovates the soul back to its state of goodness and purity. There is no true assurance in this system. You are never faithful enough. You never participate enough with God's assisting grace. As noted in chapter three, this distortion sparked the Protestant Reformation. The Bible, the ancient church, and the Reformers contended that through faith alone we receive Christ's imputed righteousness. The imputed righteousness view argued that Christ's gospel externally works redemption for the soul to deliver it out of its state of condemnation and corruption.

If our solution is Christ's internal and infusing work, then what is our problem? We are just sick in sin. With enough gracious help, we can work hard to achieve the potential blessings of union with God. We can reach peace with God, if we only are faithful enough. It is progressive and conditional.

However, since our solution is Christ's external and imputing work, then what is our problem? We are dead in sin. But God made us alive in Christ and redeemed us finally out of our condemnation and corruption. It is immediate and decisive.

Imputation does not mean we have perfect personal righteousness this side of heaven, but God credits us with a *positional* righteousness in Christ. There is nothing more we can do to increase God's desire or willingness to bless us in Christ. We have complete peace with God through faith alone in the faithful One. We are indeed saved and sanctified by faithfulness, but not our faithfulness—his.

What about the Prayer of Faith?

When considering the biblical disciplines of holiness and Christian growth, prayer seems to be one of the most faith-filled things a Christian can do. Think about it. When you pray, you are pausing to talk to the unseen God. Standing upon the promises of the written word, you speak to God with a combination of praise, confession, thanksgiving, and supplication. Your five senses cannot empirically observe God. If done by faith alone, in Christ alone, according to God's word alone, prayer should be peace-giving. It is actively, consciously resting upon the invisible God. It should not be anxiety-creating. Walking away from a time in prayer, we should not wonder if we had enough faith to lay hold of God's potential blessings. We should not wonder if God is pleased enough with our faithfulness to grant us our requests. We should not wonder if God even approves of our prayer. And we should not assume that there are the "haves" and the "have-nots"—those who know how to pray the prayer of faith and then those who do not. A priestly class and then the peasants—a karmic Christian caste system.

This distorted perspective on prayer and Christian growth is regularly misapplied to the famous passage in James:

Is anyone among you suffering? Let him pray. Is anyone cheerful? Let him sing praise. Is anyone among you sick? Let him call for the elders of the church, and let them pray over him, anointing him with oil in the name of the Lord. And the prayer of faith will save the one who is sick, and the Lord will raise him up. And if he has committed sins, he will be forgiven. Therefore, confess your sins to one another and pray for one another, that you may be healed. The prayer of a righteous person has great power as it is working. Elijah was a man with a nature like ours, and he prayed fervently that it might not rain, and for three years and six months it did not rain on the earth. Then he prayed again, and heaven gave rain, and the earth bore its fruit. (Jas 5:13–18)

If the original context is not taken into account, there are important bits of background knowledge that the modern reader can easily miss. James is writing to suffering Christians who have fled persecution. They are under immense pressure from external persecution. And within the church they backbite and devour one another. Nothing seems secure or safe. They are suffering under great anxiety, fear, and spiritual weakness. When surveying this epistle, it is obvious that James is writing to a church comprised mainly of Jewish-background believers. This audience is apparent because James briefly refers to Old Testament themes and personalities for which he gives no explanation or introduction. For instance, in this passage alone, James quickly mentions Elijah and even anointing with oil, both of which assume prior knowledge of the Jewish Bible and worship. Elsewhere he drops the names Abraham (2:23), Rahab (2:25), and even says, "You have heard of the steadfastness of Job" (5:11), which, even among the Jews, was not the most famous story. In light of the Jewish-background audience, some of James's references will come to light.

Sick or Weak?

The first issue to address that derails so many applications of this passage is that the word "sick" doesn't refer to physical sickness. That same Greek word can be translated as "weak" or "powerless," and it can suggest spiritual weakness (cf. Rom 8:3; 1 Cor 8:9). And, when James refers to the anointing oil, since these are Jewish-background believers, he is assuming his readers know that anointing with oil in the Old Testament symbolized the goodness of the presence and blessing of the Holy Spirit.

The situation is that some are spiritually weak in the faith and struggling. They must ask the elders to pray for them to be strengthened with the blessing of the Holy Spirit. If the elders intercede by faith on behalf of the struggling, anxious Christian, then God will hear them. The elders might pray for perfect peace and a stable mind on the Lord's faithfulness: "You keep him in perfect peace whose mind is stayed on you, because he trusts in you. Trust in the LORD forever, for the LORD GOD is an everlasting rock" (Isa 26:3–4). The point is not that the power is in the prayer or faith itself. The power is in God, and prayer through trust in God is what heals the person's doubt, fear, and lack of assurance. Those who are weak and frail in faith struggle with fear for lack of assurance. Their world is falling apart, and they need assurance. This is especially true for those who are suffering constant anxiety from persecution, adversity, and strained relationships. This suffering would lead them to doubt their assurance and salvation. "Has God abandoned me? What did I do or not do to make him so displeased with me? Maybe I have bad Christian karma."

The elders pray according to faith in a way that the anxious Christian doesn't have the strength to. The fact that the passage refers to spiritual weakness and not physical sickness is evidenced by unconfessed sins possibly contributed to this spiritually frail state. This is a spiritual issue that needs prayer. Obviously, it cannot be physical because there is a promise that if the elders pray in faith, the sick person will be healed and raised up, which is New Testament language for the resurrection (e.g., Matt 26:32; John 6:40). So, if someone is not physically healed, it must be because the elders didn't have enough faith, right? That's what the karmic conclusion would be. And everyone eventually dies, so that would mean that no elders truly have enough faith. Or they are negligent and have committed pastoral malpractice. Therefore, they shouldn't be elders, and we shouldn't have churches. The logic of this interpretation falls apart.

Consider how even Paul in 2 Corinthians 12 boasted in third person about his experience of heaven, which might imply to some that Paul was one of God's elites, his super saints. Paul on numerous occasions prayed for physical healing and saw God answer his prayers. But in this situation, Paul is given a messenger of Satan to torment him and keep him humble. Paul pleads passionately with the Lord three times for relief (and these were likely long protracted seasons of earnest pleading and not just three quick prayer requests). In response to his pleading, Paul says,

> But he said to me, "My grace is sufficient for you, for my power is made perfect in weakness." Therefore I will boast all the more gladly of my weaknesses, so that the power of Christ may rest upon me. For the sake of Christ, then, I am content with weaknesses, insults, hardships, persecutions, and calamities. For when I am weak, then I am strong. (2 Cor 12:9–10)

Personal or Positional Righteousness?

But what about the effective prayer of a righteous person? Wouldn't Paul fit the bill? Surely, he was righteous enough, right? And we know his prayers were effective in healing others. Clearly the more holy we are in personal righteousness, then the more powerful we are in prayer, right? That seems to be the common application of James 5:16–18. Elijah raised a child from the dead, called fire out of heaven, and ended the drought, all because he was an exceedingly godly man. But, if we understand the context of the sick person in need of healing as referring to a spiritually weak person in need of strengthened assurance through faith, then we begin to see how Elijah fits into the context. Though he was positionally righteous through faith in the Messiah, Elijah was also a struggler. His personal righteousness (obedience, holy living, etc.) waned and wavered like ours does. In two chapters he went from the heights of spiritual triumph to the depths of spiritual despair (cf. 1 Kgs 18, 19). But his positional righteousness through faith alone was rock solid just like ours. Your positional righteousness is an immutable gift from God. The good gifts he bestows in Christ are ours forever, no matter what. He does not shift or change his mind (cf. Jas 1:16–18). What God promises, he performs. Every time.

James is saying that when we pray, we trust in the power of our positional righteousness in Messiah for our prayers to be heard, just as Elijah did. True, Elijah prayed many times, even with fervency. But that was not because he anticipated God might finally listen based upon his personal righteousness. Rather, he knew God would listen because he was positionally righteous. We would despair if the basis for answered prayer were the strength and consistency of our personal righteousness. We are all strugglers, and we need a mediator to plead for us. We need a shepherd to rescue us and carry us. Hebrews 4:15, 16 say it this way:

> For we do not have a high priest who is unable to sympathize with our weaknesses, but one who in every respect has been tempted as we are, yet without sin. Let us then with confidence draw near to the throne of grace, that we may receive mercy and find grace to help in time of need.

Does it say that once we have conquered temptation enough and achieve spiritual strength, then we can confidently draw near to the throne of power? No, not at all. It's a command that in spite of our spiritual weakness, we should confidently come close to the throne. What kind of throne? A throne of grace. For what purpose? To get more Holy Spirit power for ministry? To get reimbursed for our holy living? No. "That we may receive mercy and find grace to help in time of need." Nothing about the effectiveness of the prayer of a righteous person has to do with his personal faithfulness, worthiness, or worked-up psychological certitude called "faith." The open line of communication in prayer is effectively connected via our positional righteousness in Christ. The instrument for calling upon God is faith alone.

No one would ride in a plane and boast that there is power in sitting in a chair in the sky. The power is not the sitting in the chair. The power is in the plane. The act of resting in a chair shows that you trust in the power of the plane to deliver you through the sky to your destination. Is there power in going to the hospital to get a tumor removed? Or is the power in the surgeon to do it? The only thing a patient does is show up to the hospital, wait, and rest in the surgeon's power, wisdom, and goodness to remove the tumor.

Call upon the Name of the Lord

From the opening chapters of Genesis all the way to the book of Revelation, the people of God are often described as those who call upon the name of the Lord. Paul says in Romans 10:10, 11, "For with the heart one believes and is justified, and with the mouth one confesses and is saved. For the

Scripture says, 'Everyone who believes in him will not be put to shame.'" Our positional righteousness is through faith alone in Christ alone, and such faith might seem shameful. Apparently, it must seem naïve to put all our trust in Christ alone and not hold out with trust in ourselves just in case Christ is expecting us to pitch in too. Paul anticipates such anxiety in putting all our trust in Christ alone because he says that no one who trusts in Christ will suffer shame, but they will be raised up and vindicated as recipients of the promise in the Last Day. How do we know that this vindication is not for special saints who have extra strong faith and extraordinary faithfulness? Because Paul says, "For there is no distinction between Jew and Greek; for the same Lord is Lord of all, bestowing his riches on all who call on him. For 'everyone who calls on the name of the Lord will be saved'" (Rom 10:12, 13). God loves to bestow his rich spiritual promises upon those who are declared righteous through faith and call upon his name. They will not be disappointed. Your birthright gives you free, unlimited access to the throne of grace.

The collapsing of personal righteousness and positional righteousness has discouraged and worn out many believers. In many ways, that conflation is at the heart of our karmic conundrum. We all know the exhausting demands of karmic enoughness. It does not need to be this way. We can rest in God's promises and know that our prayers will be heard through faith alone, in Christ alone, according to God's word alone, by grace alone, for God's glory alone. God is pleased to revive our weary hearts and give us grace and mercy in times of need. He is the object of your assurance, and he is the Author and Perfector of your faith. You need not add to it or take away from it. From start to finish, our faith is all of God, to the praise of the glory of his grace.

Hymn for Reflection

"Rock of Ages"[1]

1 Rock of Ages, cleft for me,
let me hide myself in thee;
let the water and the blood,
from thy wounded side which flowed,
be of sin the double cure;
save from wrath and make me pure.

2 Not the labors of my hands
can fulfill thy law's demands;
could my zeal no respite know,
could my tears forever flow,
all for sin could not atone;
thou must save, and thou alone.

3 Nothing in my hand I bring,
simply to the cross I cling;
naked, come to thee for dress;
helpless, look to thee for grace;
foul, I to the fountain fly;
wash me, Savior, or I die.

4 While I draw this fleeting breath,
when mine eyes shall close in death,
when I soar to worlds unknown,
see thee on thy judgment throne,
Rock of Ages, cleft for me,
let me hide myself in thee.

---

1 Augustus Toplady, "Rock of Ages," https://hymnary.org/text/rock_of_ages_cleft_for_me_
let_me_hide.

Questions for Reflection

1. How were the distinctions between faith in faith and faith in faithfulness helpful for you as you think about karmic Christian growth?

2. In what ways has the discussion from James encouraged you to draw near to God in prayer?

3. What is one take-away from this chapter on Christian growth that you could share with someone else?

Chapter 5

Karma and Christian Service

Scripture for Memory
Therefore, we are ambassadors for Christ, God making his appeal through us. We implore you on behalf of Christ, be reconciled to God. For our sake he made him to be sin who knew no sin, so that in him we might become the righteousness of God. (2 Cor 5:20–21)

"So, what did you think of The Table?" Elena asked Miguel on their drive home. They were a newly married couple in the Houston area, and they were trying to find a church near their new apartment.

Miguel replied, "I don't want to bail on this one like we bailed so quickly on Transform Fellowship. But I feel like we'd be so busy if we tried to get involved. They're good people, don't get me wrong, but both places feel like beehives of activity."

Elena added, "Yeah, I like the people too. They seem really excited to make a difference. But I feel a little guilty not jumping in right away with their city transformation initiatives. I don't know if I could keep up. I kind of miss Grace Bible Church in Odessa. I always felt so refreshed by Pastor Toledo's grace-filled preaching. I never felt pressured to try to redeem the city or catalyze a justice movement. I felt the freedom to use my gifts as I was able, and I never felt guilt-tripped into making a difference. Getting married and having lots of kids were just fine. Church felt more like a family than a diversity-equity workshop or a motivational conference."

This fabled scenario is indicative of big-hearted evangelical perspectives on Christian service. And when teased out, these ideas can be very karmic. To be sure, most mean well and have genuinely noble intentions to help people and please the Lord. Others might be so snowed under with an ideological herd mentality that they don't pause to reflect. They don't think about motives, biblical principles, the meaning of words, and the consequences of ideas. We all know instinctively that words have meaning, and ideas have consequences. We are meticulous when it comes to scouring legal documents and framing contracts, and any imprecise language would require a revision. But we are much too sloppy and slipshod when it comes to biblical terminology and its implications for our Christian service. Of all things, you would think we would at least be suspicious or guarded around novel and trendy theological language that has eternal consequences. Vague, swollen language clouds the truth and obscures essential doctrines.

Much of what passes for Christian service can be likened to a sandwich that is dripping with assorted sauces—mayonnaise, mustard, barbeque sauce, horseradish, and ranch dressing. The sauce concoction so lathers up the thin slice of meat that there is no meat flavor left. It just tastes like a sloppy, chewy sauce sandwich. So much of evangelical enthusiasm has added to the simplicity of the gospel and the Great Commission. After a steady diet of the evangelical slogan sauce slathered over the simple gospel and the church's mission, we can feel quite sickly and turned off by its intense flavor and minimal nutrition.

There are two kinds of karmic perspectives that can obscure the simplicity of the gospel and Christian service: the activist and the agent. Both the cultural mandate activist and the Great Commandment agent operate according to karmic rules of engagement. Their systems implode and grind to a screeching halt generation after generation. But it is the Great Commission ambassador who testifies to Christ and his redeeming work for the world to hear. It is a restful work. It is a joyful work. And it is a fruitful work. For it is Christ's prerogative to build his church and his kingdom. The ambassador simply bears witness to Christ and his work, casts the gospel seed, and sleeps easy knowing God is sovereign. We will see how the Great Commission ambassador is the peaceful alternative to the big-hearted efforts of those who strive to enact change but anxiously wonder if they are good enough.

Cultural Mandate Activists

Many good-intentioned Christians base whole ministries and initiatives around the notion that we are to run with the baton handed to Adam in the garden. God called Adam to fill the earth and take dominion, and in popular evangelical literature, that command has been merged with God's promise to bless Abraham and thus bless the nations. So, the rationale commonly goes like this: Just as Adam was supposed to take dominion of the earth, and just as Abraham was supposed to be a blessing to the earth, so now the church is tasked with bringing shalom to the earth. The church takes dominion by being a blessing through cultural transformation that affects every sphere of society and eventually heals creation. It is the church's job to stand in the gap and heal what is broken and enact justice where systemic injustice harms the oppressed.

The fundamental errors are numerous in this karmic system of Christian service. It uploads the mission of the church with ambiguous "be a blessing" language. It often guilt-trips Christians with impossible tasks like reversing global warming, ending human trafficking, stamping out racism, bringing peace on earth, eradicating hate, and advocating equity for all the oppressed. Not only are these manifestly exhausting and incredulous, but no one could accurately measure or ensure such grandiose global transformation. Whether they are well-intentioned or just plain distracting, these social media virtue signals drain the soul of the well-meaning Christian. They might effectively mobilize youthful university students and digital nomads. But those who have children to feed, who work with their backs in a blue-collar world, and serve as the sole caretakers of aging family members, already feel overwhelmed by trying to be a blessing to their own family. For those Christians immersed in family responsibilities, the thought of transforming societal structures by being a blessing is simply unthinkable. Cultural mandate activism can easily become an immense burden to the average, struggling Christian. No parent needs a PhD in childhood development to know that human nature is like the grain in wood—you cannot easily go against the grain; you need to work with it in all its imperfections. There will be knots, but they can be made beautiful with enough patience and craftsmanship. Transformation of human nature only happens through the miracle of spiritual rebirth—a heart transplant.

This system also conflates the mission of the church with the mission of God. The mission of God is the overarching mission of all other missions in the Bible. The mission of the triune God—to redeem a people for Christ to reign as a kingdom of priests to God in a resurrected creation for eternity—was not the mission of Adam. It was not the mission of Noah. It was not the mission of Israel. And it is not the mission of the church. Moreover, Christ's mission on earth—to earn righteousness for a disobedient people through obedience to the law's demands, to absorb the wrath of God for them under the law's condemnation, to be raised for their justification, and to inaugurate the kingdom of God for them—is not the mission of the church. The mission of Christ currently in heaven—to reign as King over the nations, build his church through the proclamation of the gospel, and to subject his enemies under his feet—is not the mission of the church. When Christ returns, he will extinguish all remnants of sin and the devil; he will cause his blessings to flow far as the curse is found. And this grand restoration of all things on the new earth is not the mission of the church.

The Bible never calls the church to activism—to enact social change or cultural transformation through justice initiatives, as though the church were tasked to roll out God's revolution of earth-transforming love. Whether or not it is explicitly stated, the logic inevitably suggests that the church is at fault for not doing enough to combat racism, fix the climate emergency, promote sustainability, and jettison white heteronormativity from our shameful European, colonialist past. As ridiculous as some of this sounds to the average evangelical reader, the think tanks in academic institutions and even seminaries are increasingly adopting this kind of language and merging it with evangelical jargon. So, to keep up with the latest social trends, church leaders increasingly adopt activist language and burn out the average believer.

Being part of a bigger-than-life movement of global transformation and social change can give us an adrenaline rush, but typically this karmic siren call rides on the coattails of a narcissistic leader who knows how to manipulate the good intentions of impressionable Christians. In the end, the local church and the average Christian can never be radical enough. They can never be activistic enough. They can never promote enough causes. The world is not changing fast enough because they have not mobilized enough to change enough structures and their systemic evils.

What about hoping in the return of Christ? This activistic system tends to shy away from all such imminent-return language as if it is a cultural construct of heavenly-minded, "in-the-sweet-by-and-by," anti-intellectual Christianity. How selfish we are to just wait around for Christ to return. It is our job to be a blessing and participate in the mission of God. It is our job to usher in global shalom. We don't want to be so heavenly minded that we are no earthly good. After all, the cross was all about launching God's revolution of love to change the world. We can do it. If we just mobilize enough Christians to be a blessing, then justice will roll down like rivers. If … then, if … then. Frankly, it's exhausting, it's discouraging, and it's impossible. It's karma.

Jesus is the better Adam who has passed the test in the garden, who was lifted up like a cursed serpent on a tree, whose tree of death became our tree of life. He became the righteousness of all who would look to him and live. His resurrection opened the gates to paradise, and he is progressively taking dominion of the nations. Upon his return, all of creation will be restored, but only upon the revealing of the glory of the sons of God:

> For the creation waits with eager longing for the revealing of the sons of God. For the creation was subjected to futility, not willingly, but because of him who subjected it, in hope that the creation itself will be set free from its bondage to corruption and obtain the freedom of the glory of the children of God. (Rom 8:19–21)

God himself has subjected the created order to bondage. It's not that everything since the fall has fallen apart and that God is just trying to put it back together again with the help of the church. God has subjected it all to futility. And he will flip the switch at the revelation of the resurrected people of God in Christ's glorious return. Then, and only then, will the full blessings of God's glory fill the earth as water covers the seas. Then, and only then, will Abraham's promised blessings be fully realized.

Great Commandment Agents

In the West, there seems to be a waning commitment to classic evangelism. By *classic evangelism* I mean evangelism that actually teaches and proclaims the gospel in a way that it is received as an announcement, not as advice, not as assistance, and not as an opinion. We should not confuse the popular personal evangelism techniques of the twentieth century with the genuine gift and office of evangelism. Though we might argue that some of the previous generation's techniques are now ineffective in our anti-Christian age, we must not abandon the gift of evangelism and the office of the evangelist in order to reimagine and recreate something more palatable, socially acceptable, and winsome. Often the backlash to fundamentalist Christianity has made evangelism almost anathema in many churches. Telling the truth is out of vogue, and showing love is in style. Who wants to create an awkward moment in a conversation to "talk at" someone about the gospel when we could merely "live the gospel" instead?

Consequently, the fear of being unpopular, disliked, and shamed, drives us to innovate biblical language so we can "be strategic" with our incarnational living. And a very common way of upcycling gospel proclamation for the twenty-first century is to claim that the Great Commandment and the Great Commission are the same mission. After all, the world will know we are Christians by our love (and then they will want to join our Jesus community). We can love the world to Jesus. We are his hands. We are his feet. When the world sees our deeds of love, they see Christ. Christ set the example of how to love the world back to healing, and now it is the church's job to carry on his mission of love. Loving others by living the gospel and living the Great Commission is how we will promote human flourishing for the healing of the nations. This is how we carry on the kingdom revolution of Christ's love and justice. This is how we must transform the world.

Where the cultural mandate activists merge the mission of Adam and the mission of God with the mission of the church, the Great Commandment agents often conflate the mission of Christ on earth (as they perceive it) with the mission of the church. To be sure, none of us probably have devious motives when saying things like, "The Great Commandment and the Great Commission are two sides of the same coin," "The mission of the church is to show the world the love of Jesus," "Our mission is to be Christ to the world," "We are called to incarnate Christ's love to the world," or "Go into all the world and preach the gospel, and if necessary, use words."

Have peoples' lives been genuinely improved by individual Christians doing acts of mercy? Indeed. Have we seen holistic change occur in history where individual Christians used their vocation for the good of society? Absolutely. But, was the mission of Christ on earth handed off as the mission of the church? Not at all. We must be careful not to confuse good works with good words. Our good works adorn our good words. But they do not replace them. And they are not equivalent. "Go into all the world and preach the gospel, and if necessary, use words," makes as much sense as saying, "Go into all the world and feed the poor, and if necessary, use food."

The mission of Christ on earth was to obey the stipulations of the law and to suffer its just penalty for all those condemned and corrupted in Adam. So, Christ's mission was to perfectly, personally, and perpetually love God and love others in life, and to hang as a curse on the tree in the place of his enemies. This sacrifice was the climax of a life of love for God and sinners. The outcome of Christ's earthly mission was to fulfill all righteousness for those who would receive him and his work through trust alone. The resurrection inaugurated the kingdom. It was a one-time historical event never to be repeated. We should be careful not to conflate Christ's earthly mission with the church's mission. We don't live the gospel. Christ did. And he said, "It is finished!" There was only one incarnation, and it was not us.

The Great Commandment is the summary of all the law's demands, and it is not ours to accomplish. The gospel is not that we can be more like Christ. The gospel is not that we can love God and others. These are certainly implications of the effects of the gospel, but not the gospel altogether. The gospel is not God's assistance for restoring our souls through Christ in us. The gospel is God's announcement that he has reconciled our souls to himself through Christ for us. The gospel is not a life therapy that we use to get better. The gospel is a heart transplant through which God makes us alive. In other words, we don't live the gospel. We live in light of the gospel. We don't build the kingdom. We testify to the King who is building his kingdom. We don't build the church. We testify to the gospel as Christ builds his church.

Great Commandment agents use language that sounds like we partner with God in redeeming the world. They assert that we are partners with God in the ministry of reconciling the world in love and peace. There are some fundamental problems with this approach. First, it reflects the medieval Roman Catholic teaching that Mary was a co-redemptrix. She was part of (or partner in) Christ's priestly work on earth as our redemption.

And even still, she is part of (partner in) Christ's priestly work in heaven as our intercessor. In a similar way, the idea that Christians partner with God in redeeming, reconciling, and transforming the world through obeying the Great Commandment is a modern evangelical co-redemptrix system. Though we may not look to Mary for help with living the gospel, we look to ourselves as essential partners and agents in building the kingdom. Again, for many of us who find ourselves using this language, we are theologically inconsistent at best, and theologically illiterate at worst. But theological ideas have consequences.

Nowhere does the Bible command the people of God to build his kingdom. We simply receive the kingdom. The Bible says it is the Father's good pleasure to give us the kingdom, not to partner with us in building it. Isn't it interesting that peace is the effect of simply receiving the kingdom as a gift from God? Any other approach to getting the kingdom must be riddled with fear. How so? Look at what Jesus says: "Fear not, little flock, for it is your Father's good pleasure to give you the kingdom" (Luke 12:32). In the context of this passage, Jesus is addressing the people of God who are anxious that they might not get all that they need or want in this life. In light of the anxieties of this life, the people of God may fear that they will fail to see the kingdom, but Jesus assures them that the sovereign God will not only provide for them now but also in the kingdom. Is God's provision for them transactional and contractual? Is God providing the kingdom based upon their fulfillment of his law's stipulation? Must they love him with their *whole* heart and love others *as themselves* in order to see the kingdom finally realized? No. We don't need assistance. We need an announcement. Our benevolent Father is happy to bestow upon us the kingdom and all its benefits at no cost to us whatsoever. The Son paid for it with his life. It is ours to receive through trusting his promise. He doesn't need our help. And any help we try to give him is a sign that we don't truly trust in his grace alone.

Great Commission Ambassadors

If we are not cultural mandate activists or Great Commandment agents, what's the other option? Christ does call his people to obedience in general, and especially obedience to taking the gospel of the grace of God to all the language groups. Parting words are often some of the most important and heartfelt anyone can utter, and so it is with Christ's parting words to his church. He opens his Great Commission with assurance that he has sovereign authority over heaven and earth. He closes it with the assurance that he is always with us to the very end (Matt 28:18–20).

In light of those truths, the church should proclaim the good news of Christ crucified to the nations and train up disciples in congregations who praise the triune God for the glory of his grace. To make a disciple is to make a student or an apprentice. That's what the word "disciple" means. A disciple of Christ is someone who studies Christ, which necessitates a teacher with a body of content and a plan. A disciple is not someone who hangs out with a more mature friend and just soaks up insights through osmosis. The Jewish method of discipleship was content heavy and memorization heavy. Indeed, Christ commands disciple-makers to train disciples to *keep* his word (Matt 28:20). The word, "keep," means to guard, protect, or watch over. It can be a military term for keeping one's charge loyally. To train a disciple is to train a student to study to show himself a workman who needs not be ashamed, rightly handling the word of truth. The Great Commission is inescapably church-oriented—baptizing disciples into churches. The Great Commission is unapologetically doctrine-oriented—baptizing disciples in the name of the Father and of the Son and of the Holy Spirit. The Great Commission is decisively apologetic-oriented—teaching these baptized disciples to keep, guard, and watch over the word of Christ.

We are ambassadors of a gracious king in a temporary season of amnesty. The inaugurated kingdom was announced on a bloody Roman cross two thousand years ago, upending the millennia of the devil's tyranny, and putting death to death by the death of Christ. The fullness of the kingdom will come with the King when he returns in glory. He will not come in peace next time. He will come as a just sovereign who has meticulously tracked every treasonous thought, word, and deed. The streets of the world will run red with the bloodshed of those who do not bow the knee and receive his free offer of grace and mercy. But until then, the ambassador's proclamation is, "Peace! Hear ye, hear ye, the King wishes to grant unconditional reconciliation to all who would lay down their arms. They must trust only in him and receive his free gift of grace. They will be adopted as co-heirs with him in his Father's family." Paul says,

All this is from God, who through Christ reconciled us to himself and gave us the ministry of reconciliation; that is, in Christ God was reconciling the world to himself, not counting their trespasses against them, and entrusting to us the message of reconciliation. Therefore, we are ambassadors for Christ, God making his appeal through us. We implore you on behalf of Christ, be reconciled to God. For our sake he made him to be sin who knew no sin, so that in him we might become the righteousness of God. (2 Cor 5:18–21)

There are no commands here for Great Commission ambassadors to reconcile the world to God. No commands to reconcile the world's divided factions to one another. No commands to bring shalom to creation and reconcile the world from the curse. No commands to live so lovingly and winsomely that the world is compelled to join us in loving God and loving neighbor. This text says that God reconciled (past tense) his people to himself. While we were dead in sins and trespasses, God took charge. He made the move toward us when we were hostile toward him. He sent Christ under the law to earn righteousness for his people and to suffer under the law for their unrighteousness. He passed over our guilt and imputed it to Christ. And we receive the imputation of Christ's righteousness through trusting alone in him. "If we confuse the historical, objective *content* of the gospel (Christ's redemptive work, centered in justification) with the *effects* of the gospel (Christ's redeeming work in our lives, centered in sanctification) with the *goal* of the gospel (Christ's ultimate *telos* of redemption, centered in glorification), then we will wear ourselves out with yokes of our own making."[1] We must also be mindful not to confuse the indicatives of Scripture (often promises, propositional truths, and descriptions) with its imperatives (commands and instructions for holy living). Furthermore, we must be careful not to confuse the implications of the gospel with the center of the gospel.

Therefore, our ministry of reconciliation is the message of reconciliation. Our ministry is to implore sinners to receive the message of reconciliation—God reconciled the world to himself through the blood of Christ and does not count their sins against them. The work of reconciliation was finished on the cross, and it is not ours to carry on now that Christ returned to heaven.

1   E. D. Burns, *Seeds and Stars: Resting in Christ for Great Commission Service* (Cape Coral, FL: Founders Press, 2023), 142.

Our job is to merely announce, not administer, that good news. We are not activists or agents of reconciliation. We are ambassadors of reconciliation. We can never do enough to change the world, and we can never love enough to help the world, though karmic Christianity urges us to try harder. The subversive ideas of karmic Christianity have permeated evangelical outreach and the culture of Christian service, but it doesn't need to be this way. We can remember the finished work of our gracious God, announce his terms of peace, and rest in his benevolent plan to reconcile people to himself.

After the resurrection, Christ appeared to his disciples, showed them his scarred hands and feet, and said, "Peace be with you. As the Father has sent me, even so I am sending you" (John 20:21). In other words, since God's wrath has been satisfied and death has been defeated, we have peace with God. Therefore, we go as servants and witnesses to the world because we have peace with God. We are not trying to earn or even maintain peace with God. We don't even go and serve because we have felt inner peace. We can freely, joyfully minister the gospel to the world on the basis of our objective peace with God. Christ has made peace. Fear is gone. Since we have nothing to lose, we have everything to gain.

Moreover, with all the ambiguous emphasis on being a blessing, which typically comes with meager measurable goals and assessable objectives, the truth is that we are already blessed in union with Christ. We are actually no less blessed now than we will be in the resurrection. Our spiritual blessings are enjoyed in part in this life, but in full in the next. They are in seedling form, resting dormant. Yet to substantiate our hope that the seeds of blessings are genuinely alive, they are slowly growing and partially enjoyable. As Paul makes clear in Galatians 3:15–29 and Romans 4:13–16, the blessings promised to Abraham and to those who also partake in his blessings are not based upon obedience. Otherwise, the blessings would not be of grace, but of works.

Karmic Christianity says, "Love God and others more to get blessings." The gospel says, "Since you are unconditionally blessed in the Beloved, go and love God and others with gratitude." Karmic Christianity says, "Serve the world by being a blessing so that the world will be changed." The gospel says, "Christ is the promised blessing of Abraham for all the nations. When he returns, he will make his blessings flow far as the curse is found, and the world will be changed forever." Karmic Christianity says, "As partners with God, it depends upon the church to bless the world." The gospel says, "If the blessings of God are by works, then it is no longer by faith and the promise is void."

The blessings of Zion were given by promise to Abraham and all who trust in his Seed through faith. The benefits of Sinai were proposed as potentials to Moses and all who would love God and others personally, perfectly, and perpetually. The world does not need the church to partner with God to be a blessing. Christ is the blessing of God to the world. The world needs the church to announce that blessing as received through faith alone in Christ alone. Sinners are changed by the promised blessings that come through faith—receiving grace. Sinners are not changed by the potential benefits that come through trying to live the Great Commandment—obeying the law. Grace is supernatural; it justifies sinners. The law is natural; it judges sinners.

The church's faithfulness in loving God and others is not sufficient for reconciling the world or restraining evil. God must act with special saving grace to reconcile the world. God must act with common grace to restrain evil. Karmic Christianity says, "If you love God and others, then they will be blessed." But you can never keep the Great Commandment enough. You will always fall short. You will always be left feeling anxious or exhausted or both. But the gospel says, "Since Christ loved God and others, then they will be blessed through resting in him."

Receiving the Blessed Life

Maybe more obvious than Christian living and Christian growth, karmic Christianity affects Christian service in so many ways. You can discern the karmic nature of a service/outreach initiative by noticing the conditional statements or the potentialities typically used as rallying cries and motivational tools to ignite devotion to a cause. The most important truth to remember is that the blessings of God are based upon his promise in Christ, and they are all "yes" and "amen" in Christ. Jesus is the Last Adam who inaugurated the fulfillment of the cultural mandate through his obedience, death, and resurrection. He will ultimately fulfill this royal dominion upon his return. Jesus is the Seed of Abraham, through whom all God's heavenly blessings flow to the nations. He will ultimately fulfill these ancient promises upon his return.

What God promised to Abraham, he fulfilled on Calvary. We are waiting for the fullness of those promised blessings to be progressively rolled out in this age and ultimately in the age to come. Right now, there is a hairline fracture leaking out beads of water from the dammed up reservoir of God's lavish kindness. But at the return of Christ, the dam will burst open, and deluge after deluge after deluge of benevolence will sweep us away in the ocean of God's sovereign love. This kingdom of grace is ours to receive through faith alone. We don't conceive the kingdom through our most innovative initiatives. We don't achieve the kingdom through our most faithful acts of love. We simply receive the kingdom as a gift like children enamored with the happy countenance of their Father. Fear not, it is the Father's good pleasure to give you Christ and all his benefits.

Hymn for Reflection

"The Church's One Foundation"[2]

1 The Church's one foundation
is Jesus Christ, her Lord;
she is his new creation
by water and the Word.
From heav'n he came and sought her
to be his holy bride;
with his own blood he bought her,
and for her life he died.

2 Elect from ev'ry nation,
yet one o'er all the earth;
her charter of salvation:
one Lord, one faith, one birth.
One holy name she blesses,
partakes one holy food,
and to one hope she presses,
with ev'ry grace endued.

---

2 S. J. Stone (1866), "The Church's One Foundation," https://hymnary.org/text/the_churchs_
one_foundation.

3 The Church shall never perish.
Her dear Lord to defend,
to guide, sustain, and cherish,
is with her to the end.
Tho' there be those that hate her
and strive to see her fail,
against both foe and traitor
she ever shall prevail.

4 Tho' with a scornful wonder
the world sees her oppressed,
by schisms rent asunder,
by heresies distressed,
yet saints their watch are keeping;
their cry goes up, "How long?"
and soon the night of weeping
shall be the morn of song.

Questions for Reflection

1. What are some examples of cultural mandate activists and Great Commandment agents that you have heard and maybe even adopted in your Christian service?

2. In what ways have you found the discussion about Great Commission ambassadors to be helpful and encouraging?

3. What is one take-away you could share with someone to encourage them to rest in God's promises while they serve him?

Conclusion

More Precious than Gold

Scripture for Memory
The LORD bless you and keep you; the LORD make his face to shine upon you and be gracious to you; the LORD lift up his countenance upon you and give you peace. (Num 6:24–26)

Like a faint sprinkle before a storm on the sea, the blessings we receive in this life are mere foretastes of grace to remind us that the promises of God in Christ are true but not yet realized. Though not everyone receives the same in this life, we all will be swallowed up in wave after wave of God's goodness in the resurrection. The downpour of benevolence is on the horizon. It has been storing up since before the foundation of the world for those whom God has adopted in love.

> Blessed be the God and Father of our Lord Jesus Christ, who has blessed us in Christ with every spiritual blessing in the heavenly places, even as he chose us in him before the foundation of the world, that we should be holy and blameless before him. In love he predestined us for adoption to himself as sons through Jesus Christ, according to the purpose of his will, to the praise of his glorious grace, with which he has blessed us in the Beloved. (Eph 1:3–6)

Does God act powerfully in this age to heal and miraculously bless? Of course. Is that the normal Christian life we should expect if we have enough faith and faithfulness? Not at all. The normal Christian life is one of exile in Babylon, one of traversing through the wilderness on the way to

Canaan. Though God might miraculously provide manna and water in the desert, the Promised Land is flowing with milk and honey. The kingdom we are receiving is not of this world. It will come in its fullness when the King returns. Until then, we are nomads, strangers, exiles, and pilgrims. We have a certificate of inheritance sealed with the King's blood, but all its blessings are not yet.

The normal Christian life sits at the base of Golgotha and looks to the man hanging on the cursed tree. As looking to a bronze serpent on a pole lifted high, we look to the man of all sorrows, who became sin that we might become the righteousness of God. We look to him and live. The love and justice of God displayed on Golgotha have become our passageway into the blessings of Zion. Christ's cross was like a stake that impaled the mount of the skull; he put death to death through his death. And when the stone of his garden tomb rolled away, like a seed that died and germinated, shooting out of the cold ground emerged new life. The Last Adam has earned our way back to the blessings of the garden of God. We can once again walk with God in the cool of the garden. Because Jesus was raised from the dead for our justification, his work on the mount of death opens the only way for life. Our tree of life was his tree of death. Golgotha is the key for opening the Father's house in mount Zion. Christ's faithfulness secured those blessings. And we receive them through faith alone.

Because faith alone receives all the promised blessings that karmic Christianity seeks to achieve, faith is supremely valuable. Our adversity works for our good insofar as our faith in God becomes more durable, authentic, and proven. First Peter 1:3–7 says,

> Blessed be the God and Father of our Lord Jesus Christ! According to his great mercy, he has caused us to be born again to a living hope through the resurrection of Jesus Christ from the dead, to an inheritance that is imperishable, undefiled, and unfading, kept in heaven for you, who by God's power are being guarded through faith for a salvation ready to be revealed in the last time. In this you rejoice, though now for a little while, if necessary, you have been grieved by various trials, so that the tested genuineness of your faith—more precious than gold that perishes though it is tested by fire—may be found to result in praise and glory and honor at the revelation of Jesus Christ.

Notice God's intended purpose in our trials—that the authenticity of our faith would be proven, like gold. In this life, gold is the standard for value, riches, wealth, blessing, and overall flourishing. Yet, our proven faith is more precious than all the temporal blessings derived from having pure gold. Where gold and its power perish in this fleeting life, faith is the only means of receiving the blessings and riches of God's glory for eternity. Faith is eternal gold. Heavenly gold. The goldsmith applies pressure and heat to melt the gold, clean out any dross, and then hardens it in the form that he chooses. Then once it is fashioned, he delights in its purity and its beauty. The gold reflects his face as he rejoices in it.

A Case Study: Lazarus

Consider one of the most intriguing narratives in the Gospels. It combines many of the themes of this book: karmic misunderstandings of God's inscrutable purposes, his otherworldly kind of love, the mystery of Christian suffering, the hope of resurrection glory, and the supreme value of faith in God. This is the short story of the death of Lazarus in John 11. This retelling of the story will simply let the text do the talking, and I will make comments and observations along the way so we can see how all this fits together. The Scripture text will be italicized below.

What Motivated Jesus's Love?

> *Now a certain man was ill, Lazarus of Bethany, the village of Mary and her sister Martha. It was Mary who anointed the Lord with ointment and wiped his feet with her hair, whose brother Lazarus was ill. So the sisters sent to him, saying, "Lord, he whom you love is ill." But when Jesus heard it he said, "This illness does not lead to death. It is for the glory of God, so that the Son of God may be glorified through it." (John 11:1–4)*

What motivated Jesus's love? Glory. Notice that Jesus was motivated by the glory of God being made known. His relationship to Lazarus, Mary, and Martha was very close. He loved them like good friends. It was obvious. They called for his help because he *loved* Lazarus. And because he *loved* them and Lazarus, he was motivated by his desire that they see the glory of God. But more was going on here. From the perspective of Mary and Martha, it seemed like of all people, Jesus should come to their aid to heal Lazarus since they were so close to him. After all, their intimate friendship was so warm that Mary would even anoint Jesus and wipe his feet with her hair. Surely, Jesus would drop everything and come running to Bethany to help his friends. If he were busy, he could have at least prayed from a distance for healing. If anyone deserved Christ's blessings and miraculous provision, it would have been this family. If God had favorites, they were at the top of the list. They had good Christian karma, in other words.

What Was the Outcome of Jesus's Love?

Now Jesus loved Martha and her sister and Lazarus. So, when he heard that Lazarus was ill, he stayed two days longer in the place where he was. (John 11:5–6)

What was the outcome of Jesus's love? Suffering. These two verses are some of the most important verses in the Bible for understanding God's tough love. If we can understand what is going on here, the whole fear-mongering system of karmic Christianity falls to pieces. The result of Jesus's love for Martha and Mary is indicated by the first word in verse 6, "So." That is a massive transitional word. Read it again: "Jesus loved Martha and her sister and Lazarus. So [therefore], when he heard that Lazarus was ill, he stayed two days longer in the place where he was." What is this saying? Jesus intentionally let Lazarus die. Now if you are following this logic, you would likely ask, "How is that loving?" How could it be loving to let someone you love suffer and die when you could have helped them? Welcome to the mysterious love of God for his people. Job, Joseph, Jeremiah, Ezekiel, Elijah, Paul, and so many struggling saints throughout history have wondered the same. Let's keep tracking the narrative, and we shall see.

What Was the Reason for Jesus's Gladness?

After saying these things, he said to them, "Our friend Lazarus has fallen asleep, but I go to awaken him." The disciples said to him, "Lord, if he has fallen asleep, he will recover." Now Jesus had spoken of his death, but they thought that he meant taking rest in sleep. Then Jesus told them plainly, "Lazarus has died, and for your sake I am glad that I was not there, so that you may believe. But let us go to him." (John 11:11–15)

What was the reason for Jesus's gladness? Faith. Notice that the reason for Jesus's gladness was that the people would believe, or have faith. It delights

God when his people trust in him in spite of their pain. Jesus is not glad that you are *in* a desert. But he is glad because he can see the good land he's bringing you to *through* the desert.

For Whom Was Jesus Glad?

> Jesus said to her, "I am the resurrection and the life. Whoever believes in me, though he die, yet shall he live, and everyone who lives and believes in me shall never die. Do you believe this?" She said to him, "Yes, Lord; I believe that you are the Christ, the Son of God, who is coming into the world." (John 11:25–27)

For whom was Jesus glad? Believers. Jesus tests believers in our grief and pain. The question is, will we harden or look up? Those who do not believe will harden and turn their backs on God. But those who have genuine faith go on believing to live eternally and never die. Since Jesus has ascended to heaven and is no longer physically present with us, we rejoice in his Spirit that abides with us. "Though you do not now see him, you believe in him and rejoice with joy that is inexpressible and filled with glory, obtaining the outcome of your faith, the salvation of your souls" (1 Pet 1:8–9). It is a glad thing when we hold on by faith in Christ because he can see the outcome of our faith—the salvation of our souls in the resurrection. We should rejoice with exceeding joy. The joy of the resurrection is rushing like a freight train fully loaded with your inheritance in Christ. You can hear its sound in the distance. Nothing can stop it.

How Did Jesus Respond to His Peoples' Pain?

> When Jesus saw her weeping, and the Jews who had come with her also weeping, he was deeply moved in his spirit and greatly troubled. And he said, "Where have you laid him?" They said to him, "Lord, come and see." Jesus wept. So the Jews said, "See how he loved him!" (John 11:33–36)

How did Jesus respond to his peoples' pain? Tears. In his humanity, Jesus wept. Lest we think that God is all stoic control and no compassion, look at your Savior weep in this account of his humanity. Though we know that God is impassible, or without passions (without emotional changes and variations), yet he is full of perfect compassion all the time. Jesus is not a distant sovereign waiting for you to get your act together so he can start blessing you again. On the drive home, in the shower, or lying awake at night, when the tears flow down, your heart aches, and there is no one there to share your pain, Jesus is *El Roi*—the God who sees me (Gen 16:14–15). Not only does he see you, he understands your weakness to believe his promises in the whirlwind of the pain. "For we do not have a high priest who is unable to sympathize with our weaknesses, but one who in every respect has been tempted as we are, yet without sin" (Heb 4:15).

Why Was Jesus Grateful to the Father?

Jesus said to her, "Did I not tell you that if you believed you would see the glory of God?" So they took away the stone. And Jesus lifted up his eyes and said, "Father, I thank you that you have heard me. I knew that you always hear me, but I said this on account of the people standing around, that they may believe that you sent me." When he had said these things, he cried out with a loud voice, "Lazarus, come out." (John 11:40–43)

Why was Jesus grateful to the Father? Faith. Jesus was grateful to his Father for working faith among those who were grieving. Notice Jesus didn't thank the Father primarily for Lazarus's resurrection and the relief of their grief. He thanked the Father for showing his glory so that the people would believe. Jesus orchestrates and manages our grief so that we would be made vulnerable and look to him alone as our resurrection and our life.

Now remember the progression of the story—Lazarus is sick; Jesus loves Martha, Mary, and Lazarus; and because of his love for them, he wants them to see the glory of God; therefore he lets Lazarus die, and Mary and Martha suffer, which means that he too would suffer immense grief leading him to weep. But in spite of the grief, Jesus is glad because God's glory would be made known and his people would believe in the coming resurrection promises. This brief narrative obliterates karmic Christianity on every level.

Peace in the Silence

Our chief Shepherd desires his flock to see the glory of God, believe, and be saved forever for him. This is the gift of the kingdom. The kingdom is coming with all the blessings that you try to manufacture or maintain in this life, though you never seem to achieve all that you would like. True, habitual sins have bad consequences, and Adam's sin certainly has had ongoing consequences. But the effects of the curse and the secret providence of God in our suffering are not for us to decode in this life. The blessings of God are not for us to release from the heavenlies if we would only align ourselves in unity with God's purposes—this view is karmic Christianity, and does nothing for us other than instill fear of messing up and missing out on God's best for us. It's pagan to the core. We must renounce it by remembering the promises and resting in the Promise-Keeper. God's promises are not potentialities. God's covenant is not a contract. Don't confuse Zion with Sinai. Don't fear God's deafening silence. Sometimes God is most at work to purify your faith when life feels frozen over. The kingdom is coming by stealth, and you can be at peace knowing the darkness will certainly lift. The dawn breaks after the darkest dark. Your seed of peace is not lost. It is rooted in Golgotha. Its flower will bud in Zion. The blessings of God are received by our positional righteousness through faith alone. They are not achieved by our personal righteousness through faithfulness.

The promises of God in the gospel are for strengthening us to endure by faith, as Paul came "strengthening the souls of the disciples, encouraging them to continue in the faith, and saying that through many tribulations we must enter the kingdom of God" (Acts 14:22). Jesus knows that the Christian life is riddled with grief, pain, and struggle, and the upshot of these trials is anxiety. Fear eats like termites at the foundation of our confidence in God's promises. Let us not give up in fear or anxiously misinterpret God's purifying, yet severe providences. They are not some sort of cryptic karmic punishment for unintentional sins. Jesus consoles his trembling lambs: "Fear not, little flock, for it is your Father's good pleasure to give you the kingdom" (Luke 12:32).

Peace to you.

Hymn for Reflection

"Be Still My Soul"[1]

1 Be still, my soul; the Lord is on your side;
bear patiently the cross of grief or pain;
leave to your God to order and provide;
in ev'ry change he faithful will remain.
Be still, my soul; your best, your heav'nly friend
through thorny ways leads to a joyful end.

2 Be still, my soul; your God will undertake
to guide the future as he has the past;
your hope, your confidence, let nothing shake;
all now mysterious shall be bright at last.
Be still, my soul; the waves and winds still know
his voice who ruled them while he lived below.

3 Be still, my soul; when dearest friends depart
and all is darkened in the vale of tears,
then you will better know his love, his heart,
who comes to soothe your sorrows and your fears.
Be still, my soul; your Jesus can repay
from his own fullness all he takes away.

4 Be still, my soul; the hour is hast'ning on
when we shall be forever with the Lord,
when disappointment, grief, and fear are gone,
sorrow forgot, love's purest joys restored.
Be still my soul; when change and tears are past,
all safe and blessed we shall meet at last.

---

1 Kathrina von Schlegel, translated by Jane Borthwick, "Be Still, My Soul," https://hymnary.
org/text/be_still_my_soul_the_lord_is_on_thy_side.

Questions for Reflection

1. How did the narrative of Lazarus impact your understanding of God's purposes in our pain?

2. In what ways did the story of Lazarus tie together some of the themes discussed in previous chapters?

3. How has the Lord encouraged you through his word to rest in his promises?

Acknowledgments

I wish to thank those ministry supporters, churches, students, pastors, and friends who have encouraged me over the years to put together this book. I'm grateful to the faculty at Asia Biblical Theological Seminary for their support. I am indebted to my parents, sister, and extended family who have always been so encouraging and supportive of my writing.

Most of all, I wish to thank my faith-filled, courageous, and affectionate sons, Elijah and Isaiah. Your enthusiasm and unending encouragement for my writing and teaching have left me speechless. I am unworthy to be your father. May you trust in Christ above all. He will be your stability and peace at all times.

Blessed is the man who trusts in the LORD, whose trust is the LORD. He is like a tree planted by water, that sends out its roots by the stream, and does not fear when heat comes, for its leaves remain green, and is not anxious in the year of drought, for it does not cease to bear fruit." (Jer 17:7–8)

WILLIAM CAREY PUBLISHING
visit us at missionbooks.org

The Only One: Living Fully In, By, and For God
Curtis Sergeant | Paperback & ePub

Designed to be read, processed, shared, and used to equip others, *The Only One* is a tool to not only grow as a disciple but also to make and multiply disciples. This is about living with a greater impact on the world and the purpose for which God designed you. It's time to experience life with Him, and others, as a joyful and exciting adventure—read this book and get started!

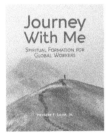

Journey With Me: Spiritual Formation for Global Workers
Herbert F. Lamp, Jr. | Paperback & ePub

Journey With Me illustrates that ministry is the result of the overflow of our relationship with God, rather than vice versa. Exploring over fifteen ancient spiritual graces—such as Lectio Divina, rule of life, silence and solitude, and prayer of Examen—Herbert F. Lamp, Jr. invites us to prioritize soul care, rather than treating ministry as a replacement for intimacy. In the process of knowing and being known, God fills us up with his love, joy, peace, and wisdom. Only then can we minister to others, balancing a heart for God with hands for service.

Spirit Walk (Special Edition): The Extraordinary Power of Acts of Ordinary People
Steve Smith | Paperback & ePub

Though we know the Bible says to walk in the Spirit, the majority of Christians are illiterate about how to practically live in His power. The result is lives marred by continued brokenness and ministries plagued by fruitlessness. In contrast, believers from Acts understood the ancient path of the Spirit Walk. That extraordinary power was not just for them, but also for us. Gleaning insights from implementation in dozens of Acts-like movements around the world, *Spirit Walk* takes you through the timeless principles of the Bible.

CPSIA information can be obtained
at www.ICGtesting.com
Printed in the USA
LVHW012212260723
753604LV00011B/293

9 781645 085072